Designing and Drawing Tessellations

"Geese" © 2000 Robert Fathauer

Designing and Drawing Tessellations

Robert Fathauer

Tessellations
Phoenix, Arizona

ISBN 978-0-9802191-3-5

Printed in the United States of America

Contents

Preface

It's been nearly twenty years since I designed my first Escheresque tessellation, a process that I found very challenging. Like many complex tasks, designing and drawing tessellations becomes much easier with practice and repetition. One of the reasons I wrote this book was to share what I've learned over the last two decades. Earlier books that describe how to create Escheresque tessellations are geared at teaching novices how to create basic designs. While this book assumes no prior experience with tessellations and covers the basics in depth, the goal is to equip the interested reader, teacher, student, and artist with the tools needed to fully realize his or her potential with this fascinating art form.

The first two chapters of this book provide background, with some history of the topic and examples of tessellations in the world around us. Chapters 3 and 4 describe the mathematics behind tessellations, the concepts and terminology, and how symmetry makes them possible. Chapters 5 and 6 are more concerned with the artistic side, describing techniques for creating effective designs. Chapters 7 through 11 walk the reader through the process of creating tessellations, and contain numerous templates for different types of tessellations. Activities written for a classroom setting are found at the end of each chapter, but these can also be used by individuals.

Designing and drawing tessellations is a task that combines two of my great loves, art and mathematics. Part of it is like solving a puzzle, and it has that addictive aspect of good puzzles. Another part of it is creative expression, which can be deeply satisfying. The hope is that this book will help others enjoy this activity as much as I have.

I would like to acknowledge a few of the people whose work made this book possible. It was the art of M.C. Escher that led me down this path, and I have spent many enjoyable hours studying his fascinating tessellations and prints. Doris Schattschneider's book *M.C. Escher: Visions of Symmetry* was very helpful in understanding Escher's work and learning how to create my own tessellations. Finally, Branko Grünbaum and G.C. Shephard's book *Tilings and Patterns* has been an invaluable resource that I have turned to time and time again.

Robert Fathauer
Phoenix, Arizona, December, 2008

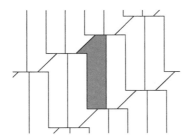

Introduction to Tessellations

A tessellation is a collection of shapes that fit together without gaps or overlaps to cover the infinite mathematical plane. Another word for tessellation is tiling, and the individual shapes in a tessellation are referred to as tiles. In a more general sense, a tessellation covers any surface, not necessarily flat or infinite in extent. In this sense, tessellations are found in all cultures from very early on. They are used in many practical applications like tiling a floor or decorating pots or cloth.

The word tessellation is sometimes used to specifically refer to tilings in which the individual tiles are recognizable, real-world motifs. The subject of this book is the design of this sort of tessellation, These will sometimes be referred to as Escheresque tessellations (after M.C. Escher), and the tiles in them Escheresque tiles. These sorts of designs are a relatively recent phenomenon, dating back a little over a century.

Historical Examples of the Use of Tessellations

The word tessellation comes from the Greek word *tessares*, meaning four, and the Latin *tessellare*, meaning to pave with tesserae. Tessera (plural form tesserae), are small squares or cubes of stone or glass used for creating mosaics.

The Ancient Romans often used tesserae to form larger tessellations, as well as figures such as animals or people. In addition, they used geometric tiles like rhombi (diamonds) to form tessellations as decorative floor coverings. The examples shown here are all from Pompeii, Italy.

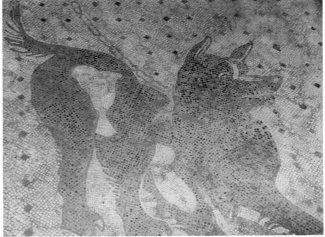

Tessellations have long been used in brickwork. The Ancient Romans made use of fired bricks. The photo at right shows the brickwork in an ancient tomb on the Appian Way in Rome.

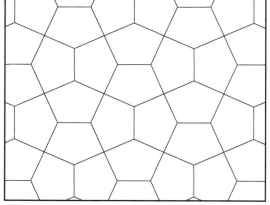

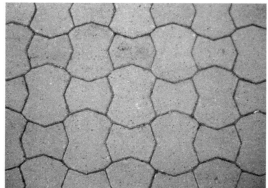

Another early and widespread use of tessellations was in laying paving stones. A common street paving in Cairo, Egypt is shown above left. It is notable for the interesting tessellation formed by pentagons, four of which form larger hexagons, with hexagon patterns running in two different directions. Contemporary paving stones seen in Rahden, Germany are shown below it.

Many examples of tessellations can be found in European cathedrals and castles dating back several centuries. The example at right shows a mosaic from the floor of Saint-Sernin Basilica, a Romanesque building in Toulouse, France. The small tiles of the mosaic are used to build larger patterns that can be considered tessellations. The stonework below, based on a tessellation of hexagons, is found in St. Paul's Cathedral in London.

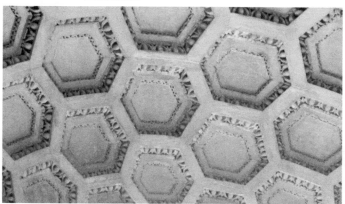

Rich and complex tessellations are common in Islamic art and architecture, which flourished from the 9th through 16th centuries. These decorative elements can be profuse in Moorish palaces such as the Alhambra, in Granada, Spain, and in mosques throughout the Middle East and beyond. Some examples are shown below.

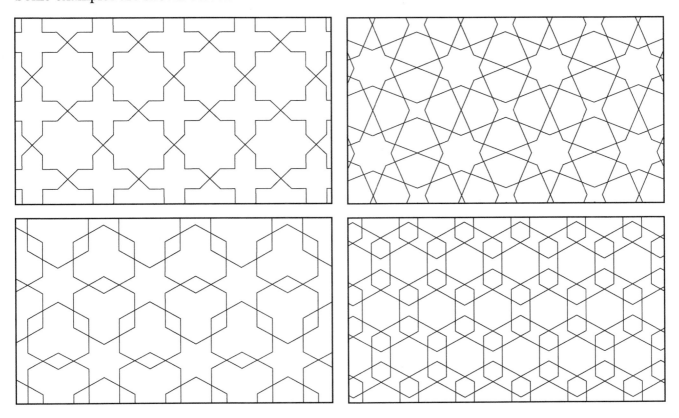

During the Renaissance, artists and mathematicians alike were fascinated by polyhedra and tessellations. Albrecht Dürer (1471-1528), a painter and printmaker, designed a tessellation incorporating pentagons and rhombi. Johannes Kepler (1571-1630), most famous for discovering the laws of planetary motion, designed tessellations of regular and star polygons, including those shown below and at right, from his 1619 book *Harmonices Mundi*.

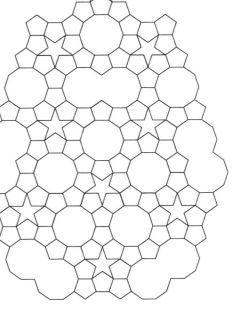

Koloman Moser

Lifelike motifs were incorporated early on in decorative patterns and designs, and some of these might be considered tessellations. However, Koloman Moser, an Austrian designer and artist who lived from 1868 to 1918, is generally credited with creating the first tessellations in which the individual tiles depict recognizable, real-world objects. In addition to painting, Moser designed jewelry, glass, ceramics, furniture, and more. He was dedicated to fine craftsmanship and his work incorporated stylized versions of forms found in nature.

The tessellations shown here were published in 1901-1902 as part of a work titled "Die Quelle". While the leaf tessellation possesses simple translational symmetry, the crow tessellation employs the more sophisticated glide reflection symmetry described in Chapter 4.

M.C. Escher

M.C. Escher is the name most often associated with tessellations in which the tiles are recognizable motifs. Escher was a Dutch graphic artist who lived from 1898 to 1972. Early in his career, his work depicts landscapes and other conventional themes. He became fascinated with tessellations when he visited the Alhambra, a Moorish palace in Granada, Spain, in 1922, and made drawings of several of the geometric tessellations he saw there. He also made drawings of the tilings on the Twelfth-century pulpit (see close-up photo below) of the cathedral in Ravello, Italy, where he spent time in the 1920's. His first tessellations in which the tiles were recognizable motifs were made in 1926-1927, and in 1936 he began producing a large number of such designs. He kept notebooks in which he enumerated 137 of these designs and recorded his own classification system for them. His notebooks are meticulously reproduced and analyzed in Doris Schattschneider's book *Visions of Symmetry – Notebooks, Periodic Drawings, and Related Woks of M. C. Escher*. He remained fascinated by these sorts of designs for the remainder of his life, with his last numbered design being produced in 1971. In the chapters with tessellation templates later in this book, there are several notes on designs of Escher's that can be created with the templates.

Escher incorporated many of his tessellations into woodcuts and lithographs that became well known. Some of the most popular of these involve the metamorphosis of tessellations from geometric tiles to real-world motifs. Others play on the two-dimensional nature of tessellations and the three-dimensional nature of our world. For example, in his 1943 lithograph "Reptiles", a tessellation of reptiles drawn of paper is shown. At one edge, the reptiles become three-dimensional, crawl out of the paper, make a circuit and crawl back in on the other side.

More recent work

Escher's tessellations have inspired many mathematicians and artists. Starting roughly around 1990, several artists put considerable time and effort into designing their own tessellations in which the tiles are real-world motifs. Prior to that time, there were only scattered attempts at such designs. These artists include Andrew Crompton, Hop David, Robert Fathauer, Ken Landry, Makoto Nakamura, John Osborn, and Peter Raedschelders. Examples of their work can be seen on the World Wide Web (see the bibliography for url's).

Some of these artists have pushed tessellations in new directions not explored by Escher. John Osborn and Robert Fathauer have created Escheresque tiles that can be assembled in many different ways, following Sir Roger Penrose's creation of a hen design for his famous aperiodic tiles. These designs have been used as the basis for puzzles. Peter Raedschelders and Robert Fathauer have created fractal tessellations using Escheresque tiles. Fractals are a branch of mathematics that was only brought to light near the end of Escher's life. Ken Landry has applied his tessellations to the surfaces of complex polyhedra, following similar application of Escher's designs in the 1977 book *M.C. Escher Kaleidocycles*, by Doris Schattschneider and Wallace Walker.

Polyominoes and related tiles

In addition to their decorative and utilitarian uses, tessellations are popular in recreational mathematics. Polyominoes were "invented" in the 1950's by Solomon Golomb, an American mathematician. A polyomino is a shape made up of squares attached in edge-to-edge fashion. These shapes have been very popular in recreational mathematics as well as in education. There are five different tetrominoes, shapes made up of four squares, and these are the shapes used in the computer game Tetris, designed by Russian computer engineer Alexey Pajitnov in 1985. In Tetris, falling tetrominoes have to be oriented and positioned to fit into a growing tessellation. In schools, pentominoes have been widely used for teaching about math and problem solving. These are comprised of five squares, and there are twelve distinct pentominoes.

Analogous families of shapes based on other polygons have been invented as well. Polyhexes are shapes made up of regular hexagons attached in edge-to-edge fashion, and polyiamonds are shapes made up of equilateral triangles attached in edge-to-edge fashion. Examples of two different pentomino tessellations are shown below.

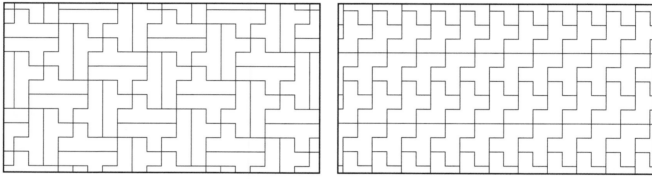

Penrose, Ammann, and non-periodic tessellations

Tessellations are also a topic studied by mathematicians. In 1966, R. Berger made the counterintuitive discovery of the first set of tiles that would admit infinitely many tilings of the plane, none of which are periodic, or repeating. It had previously been conjectured that no such set existed. Early sets of this sort had many different tiles, but in 1973/4 English theoretical physicist Sir Roger Penrose discovered sets with as few as two tiles. One version of these, known as "kites and darts", are shown below, left. The tiles have matching rules that prevent periodic arrangements (see p. 142 for information on a puzzle based on these tiles). About the same time, and independently, Robert Ammann, an American Postal Office employee and amateur mathematician, discovered related sets of non-periodic tiles. One of these is shown below, right, with markings that enforce the matching rules.

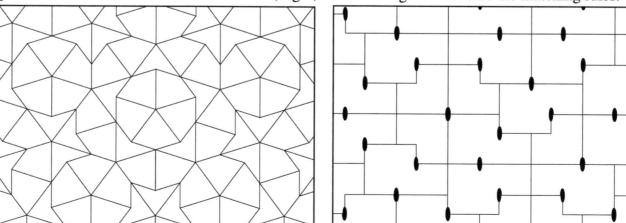

Tessellations and Mathematics Education

Over the course of the 1990's, tessellations became widely taught in schools. There were several contributing factors behind this. One is that teachers became aware of the educational value of teaching tessellations, particularly for the math content (see below). At the same time, teachers realized that students love tessellations. When students are excited about an activity, they learn more effectively. In parallel, books and software appeared on the market that facilitated the understanding and use of tessellations. The 1989 book *Introduction to Tessellations*, by Dale Seymour and Jill Britton helped raise awareness of tessellations and make the topic more accessible. M.C. Escher's tessellations were published in full for the first time and analyzed in the 1990 book *Visions of Symmetry – Notebooks, Periodic Drawings, and Related Works of M.C. Escher*, by Doris Schattschneider. A 1994 computer program called *TesselMania!*, written by Kevin Lee, made it easier for students to design their own tessellations. In 1993, my own company, called Tessellations, produced its first tessellation puzzle, *Squids & Rays*.

The National Council of Teachers of Mathematics (NCTM) published *Principles and Standards for School Mathematics* in 2000, detailing the content that math teachers should be imparting to their students at different grade levels. There are four geometry standards for grades K-12, and all of these are addressed in this book, as detailed below. In addition, standards for problem solving and connections are addressed. Classroom activities at the end of each chapter reinforce the material in the chapter that addresses these standards.

Geometry Standard: Analyze characteristics and properties of two- and three-dimensional geometric shapes and develop mathematical arguments about geometric relationships.
How it's addressed: In Chapter 3, various types of polygons are described, and examples are presented of tessellations created using them.

Geometry Standard: Specify locations and describe spatial relationships using coordinate geometry and other representational systems.
How it's addressed: In Chapter 3, a notation for describing vertices of tiles as well as tessellations is presented. In addition, two classification systems for tessellations and patterns are described in Chapter 4.

Geometry Standard: Apply transformations and use symmetry to analyze mathematical situations.
How it's addressed: In Chapter 4, the use of transformations to form tessellating tiles is described, as well as the types of symmetry in isolated objects and in tessellations.

Geometry Standard: Use visualization, spatial reasoning, and geometric modeling to solve problems.
How it's addressed: Chapters 7-11 teach the design and drawing of tessellations using various templates. The exercise of designing an Escheresque tessellation is a problem-solving exercise requiring visualization, spatial reasoning, and geometric stylization of natural motifs.

Problem Solving Standard: Solve problems that arise in mathematics and in other contexts.
How it's addressed: Designing tessellations is problem solving, and not solely in the realm of mathematics, but involving art and nature as well.

Connections Standard: Recognize and apply mathematics in contexts outside of mathematics.
How it's addressed: The topic of this book is the design and drawing of tessellations in which the tiles are real-world motifs. I.e., the entire book is concerned with using mathematics to create art. In addition, Chapter 2 is about recognizing tessellations that are present in manmade and natural objects.

Activities

Activity 1-1. Recognizing tessellations

Throughout the book, the activities are worded for teachers working with students. However, the activities can also be carried out by individuals, who can answer the discussion questions after completing each activity.

Materials: Copies of the worksheet.

Objective: Learn to tell if a collection of shapes is a tessellation or not.

Vocabulary: Tessellation, infinite, mathematical plane.

Activity Sequence:
1. Write the definition of a tessellation on the board. Be sure the class understands it, and also what the terms infinite and mathematical plane mean.
2. Pass out copies of the worksheet.
3. Have the students circle those patterns that are tessellations, and put an "X" through those that aren't.

Discussion Questions:
1. Is pattern letter a/b/c/d/e/f a tessellation?
2. Why or why not?
3. If it isn't, how might it be changed to make it into a tessellation?

Activity 1-2. Historical tessellations

Materials: Copies of the worksheet.

Objective: Learn about the variety of tessellations from different time periods and cultures.

Vocabulary: Islamic, star polygon, tessera, motif, Middle Ages, rhombus.

Activity Sequence:
1. Write the vocabulary terms on the board and discuss the meaning of each.
2. Pass out copies of the worksheet.
3. Have the students draw lines connecting the word descriptions to the representative tessellations.

Discussion Questions:
1. Which tessellation corresponds to the first word description? How do you know?
2. Which tessellation corresponds to the second word description? How do you know?
3. Which tessellation corresponds to the third word description? How do you know?
4. Which tessellation corresponds to the fourth word description? How do you know?
5. Which tessellation corresponds to the fifth word description? How do you know?
6. Which tessellation corresponds to the sixth word description? How do you know?

Worksheet 1-1. Recognizing tessellations

Circle the collections of gray squares that are tessellations; "X" through those that aren't.

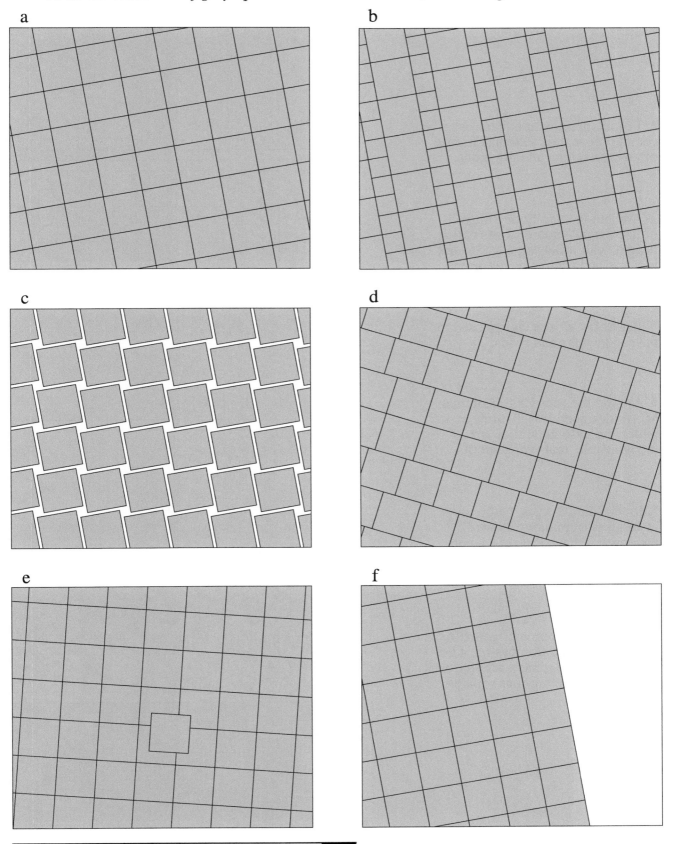

a

b

c

d

e

f

Worksheet 1-2. Historical tessellations

Draw lines to match the paragraph describing the use of tessellations in various times and cultures at left with the representative examples at right.

1. Islamic architecture features complex geometric tessellations that often incorporate star polygons.

2. Ancient Roman floor tilings utilized small square stones called tessera, with which larger geometric patterns and figures were formed.

3. Bricks have been widely used to pave sidewalks and roads.

4. Around the year 1900, Koloman Moser designed tessellations in which the individual tiles are recognizable, real-world motifs.

5. In the Middle Ages, before large plate glass technology existed, windows were made up of a number of small square, rectangular, or rhombus-shaped panes.

6. "Tetris" is a computer game in which falling tetrominoes must be fit together. Tetrominoes are shapes made by connecting four squares.

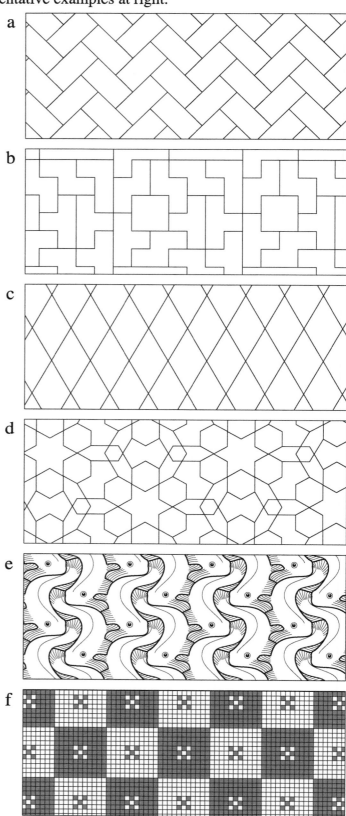

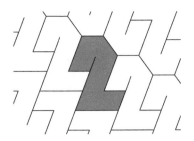

Tessellations in Our World

Tessellations are all around us and play an important role in our daily lives. They are seen both in the natural world and in things made by people.

Tessellations are widely used for decoration – of cloth, pots, wallpaper, masks, etc. In these applications, people use tessellation to make surfaces more beautiful or more interesting. Tessellations are also widely used for utilitarian, or practical, purposes. In these applications, it is often the case that dividing up a large structure into smaller building blocks makes it easier to fabricate that structure. Examples include a wall made of bricks or blocks, the weaving of a basket, the shingles of a roof, and the panes of a window. Note that there are often decorative aspects to these utilitarian uses. For example, floor tiles can be laid in attractive patterns.

As with tessellations designed by people, tessellations in nature are often used to cover a surface (e.g., the scales on a snake) or to form a barrier (e.g., a spider web). The breaking up of a continuous layer into individual pieces (e.g., the cracking of mud) can be a stress-relief mechanism. A layer of cells in a plant is another example of dividing up a plane into tiles.

A tessellation is a mathematical construction in which the individual tiles meet along a line of zero width. In any real-world tessellation there will be some finite width to that line. In addition, no real-world plane is perfectly flat. Nor is any real shape perfectly geometric; e.g., no brick is a perfect rectangle. Finally, any real-world tessellation will obviously have finite extent, while a mathematical tessellation extends to infinity. When we talk about tessellations in the real world, then, it should always be kept in mind that we are talking about something that does not strictly meet the definition of a tessellation given in Chapter 1. Another way of looking at it is that the tessellation that we associate with a physical object is a mathematical model that approximates something in the real world.

The following pages provide several examples of tessellations in the world around us. In some cases, a drawing shows a portion of a geometric tessellation that is approximated by the real world object. This sort of approximating, or modeling, is a key way scientists employ mathematics to help understand the physical universe. Learning to recognize mathematics in the world around us helps us to better understand the world in which we live. A classroom poster titled *Tessellations in Our World* is available that provides a number of examples (see p. 142 for more information).

The veins in a dragonfly's wing are an example of a tessellation found in nature.

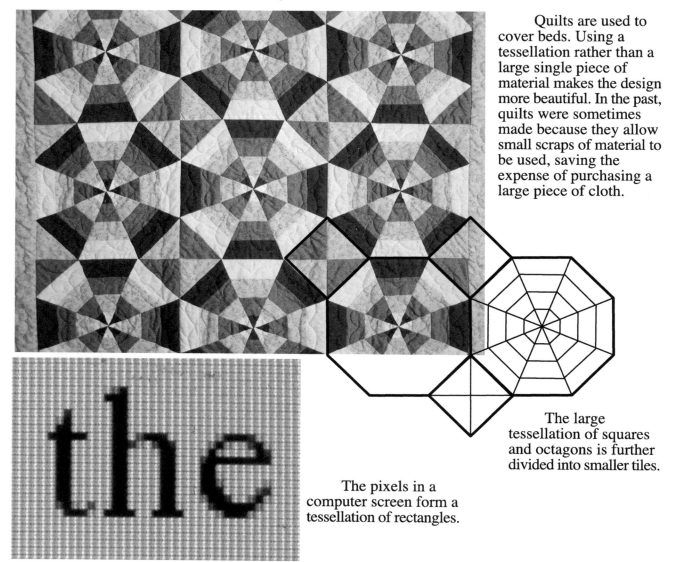

Quilts are used to cover beds. Using a tessellation rather than a large single piece of material makes the design more beautiful. In the past, quilts were sometimes made because they allow small scraps of material to be used, saving the expense of purchasing a large piece of cloth.

The large tessellation of squares and octagons is further divided into smaller tiles.

The pixels in a computer screen form a tessellation of rectangles.

Weaving makes it possible to form rounded baskets out of flat, narrow strips of plant matter such as grass. Decorating baskets with areas of different color makes them more beautiful. In the African basket shown here, a large tessellation of zigzags and diamonds is broken into squares in some areas. Each square consists of three small strips of material.

Bricks are used for sidewalks, roads, and walls. The tessellations formed by them make these surfaces more interesting. The four examples of brickwork shown here are all from the Netherlands.

A net serves as a barrier to keep children safe as they play. The tiles of this tessellation are the open spaces that allow people to see in and out.

The veins in a leaf carry water up from the roots. They divide the leaf into small portions that can be seen as tiles, so that no portion of the leaf is too far from a source of water. These tiles can be modeled as an irregular tessellation of polygons.

An orange slide is divided into wedges, and each of these is divided into smaller cells that can be modeled as a tessellation of polygons, as shown in the lower zoom by white lines.

As water leaves mud during drying, it contracts. The resultant stress causes the mud to crack. This structure can be modeled as an irregular tessellation of tiles with straight and curved edges.

Scales provide a flexible protective covering for animals like lizards (right and above) and fish (below).

Some spiders webs possess considerable symmetry, but some, like this one, form a jumble of polygons.

Activity 2-1. Building with tessellations

Materials: Copies of Worksheet 2-1.

Objective: Learn how tessellations can be used to add beauty to utilitarian structures.

Vocabulary: Utilitarian.

Activity Sequence:
1. Write the vocabulary term on the board and discuss its meaning.
2. Pass out the worksheets.
3. Have students draw tessellations as instructed on the worksheet.
4. Ask students to share some of their designs.

Discussion Questions:
1. Which of your three designs is your favorite?
2. Why do you like it?
3. What features do you think make for a good design?

Activity 2-2. Modeling natural tessellations using geometric tessellations

Materials: Copies of Worksheet 2-2.

Objective: Learn to see geometric underpinnings of less regular, natural tessellations.

Vocabulary: Mathematical modeling, geometric tessellation, natural tessellation.

Activity Sequence:
1. Write the vocabulary terms on the board and discuss the meaning of each one.
2. Pass out the worksheets.
3. Have students draw tessellations as instructed on the worksheet.
4. Ask students to share some of their designs.

Discussion Questions:
1. Which did you find more difficult, drawing the more naturalistic tessellation or simplifying it into a more regular geometric tessellation? Why?
2. Why do you think tessellations occur in nature?
3. What are some of the functions that tessellations accomplish in nature?
4. Can you think of some additional examples of tessellations in nature?

Worksheet 2-1. Building with tessellations

Imagine you have two different types of bricks with which to pave a driveway, one square and one rectangular, as shown. Using the grid provided, design three different tessellations for doing this that use both types of bricks. Try to make interesting and attractive designs.

Worksheet 2-2. Modeling natural tessellations using geometric tessellations

For each real-world object, first draw a portion as a tessellation of tiles that are close to the photograph in shape, and then as a more geometrically-regular tessellation, as shown in the example.

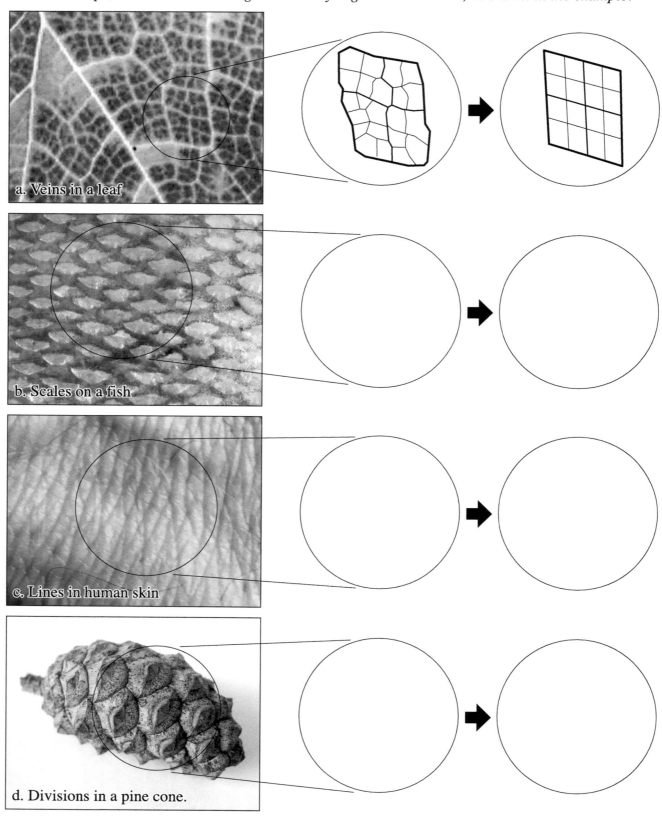

a. Veins in a leaf

b. Scales on a fish

c. Lines in human skin

d. Divisions in a pine cone.

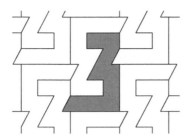

Geometric Tessellations

In order to explore tessellations more fully, it will be helpful to have a better understanding of the mathematics behind them. Recall that a tessellation is a collection of shapes, called tiles, that fit together without gaps or overlaps to cover the infinite plane.

Tiles

Let's look more closely at tiles. A mathematical definition of a tile is a closed topological set. In simpler terms, a tile is a set whose boundary is a single simple closed curve. In this context, the term curve includes straight line segments, so basically any single two-dimensional shape without holes is a tile. Tiles also shouldn't neck down to points or lines anywhere. The area inside the curve, or boundary, is the interior of the tile. The figures below show some examples of things that are not tiles: (a) a collection of unconnected shapes, (b) two shapes touching at a point, and (c) a shape with a hole in it.

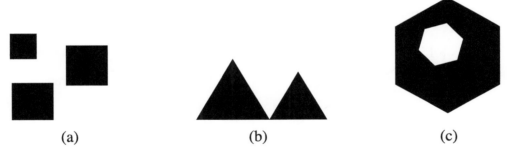

(a)   (b)   (c)

A polygon is a closed plane figure made up of straight-line segments. For a polygonal tile, the individual segments are referred to as edges, and the points where two edges meet are referred to as corners.

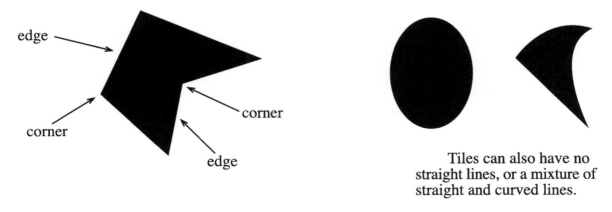

edge

corner

corner

edge

Tiles can also have no straight lines, or a mixture of straight and curved lines.

Angles

For a polygonal tile, the angle between two adjacent edges inside the tile is called the interior angle. The angle between the same two edges outside the tile is called the exterior angle. A full revolution measures 360°. As a result, for any two adjacent edges of a tile, the interior and exterior angles always sum to 360°.

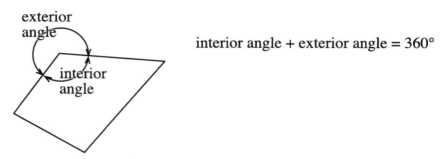

interior angle + exterior angle = 360°

Some common angles encountered in tessellations are shown below. Each angle is specified in three different ways: in degrees, as a fraction of π, and as a fraction of a full revolution. A full revolution equals 360° or 2π.

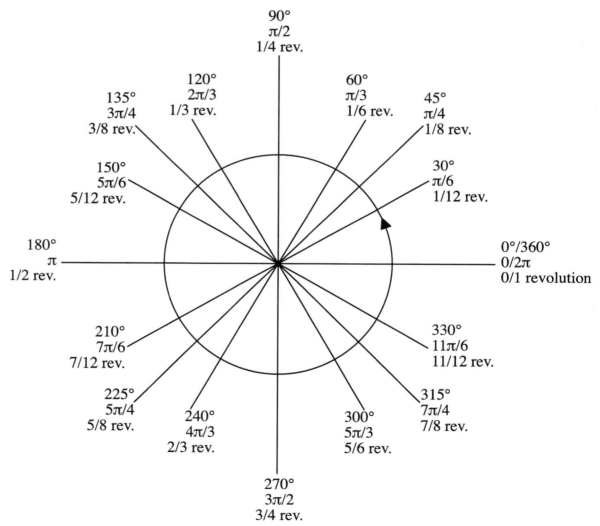

Vertices and Edge-to-edge Tessellations

A point at which three or more tiles meet is called a vertex. The sums of the interior angles of the tiles meeting at a vertex must be 360°, which is a full revolution. Some examples are given below.

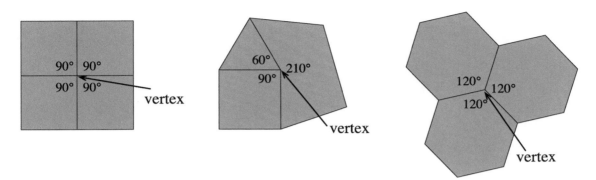

A tessellation of polygons is called edge-to-edge if adjacent tiles always touch along their entire edges. In other words, the corners of the tiles coincide with the vertices of the tessellation. The top two tessellations below are edge-to-edge, but the bottom two are not. Since one of the requirements of a tessellation is that it covers the infinite mathematical plane, the drawings below just show finite portions of infinite tessellations.

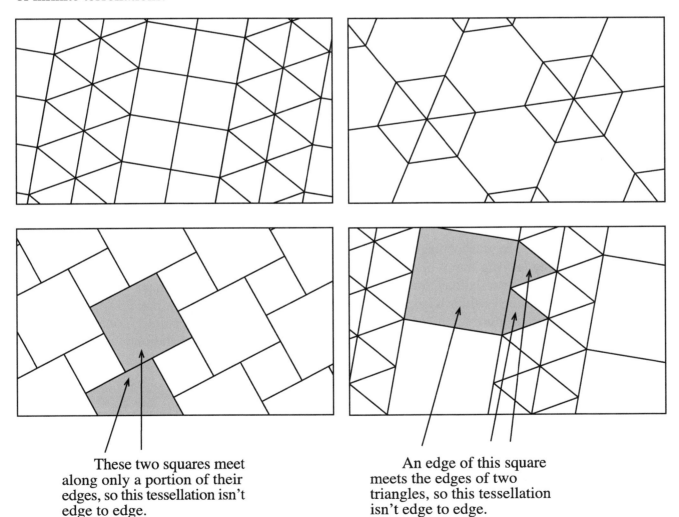

These two squares meet along only a portion of their edges, so this tessellation isn't edge to edge.

An edge of this square meets the edges of two triangles, so this tessellation isn't edge to edge.

Regular Polygons and Regular Tessellations

A regular polygon is one for which each edge is of the same length, and each interior angle has the same value. Some regular polygons are shown below that are found in a variety of tessellations. Their names and interior angles are given. All of these shapes are included in a Tessellations puzzle called *Tessel-gons* (see page 142).

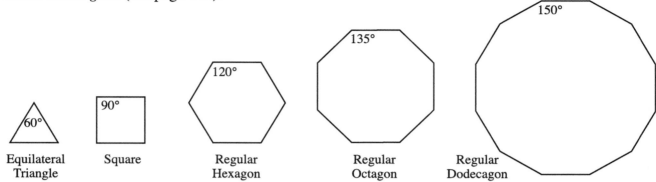

| Equilateral Triangle | Square | Regular Hexagon | Regular Octagon | Regular Dodecagon |

There are three regular tessellations – edge-to-edge tessellations for which each tile is the same type of regular polygon, as shown here.

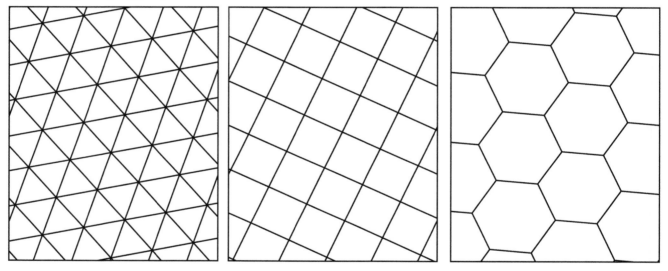

As shown below, regular pentagons do not tessellate, as it is not possible for them to meet at a point without either leaving a gap or overlapping. Since equilateral triangles, squares, and regular hexagons form regular tessellations, that takes care of regular polygons through six sides. Any regular polygon with more than six sides has interior angles greater than 120°, and since 360°/3 = 120°, it's not possible for three or more of any of these regular polygons to meet at a point. Triangles, squares, and hexagons are therefore the only regular polygons that form regular tessellations.

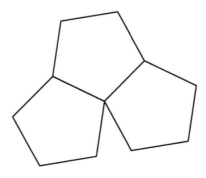

Types of Vertices

Vertices are characterized by the types of tiles that meet at them. If the same types of tiles meet at two vertices and in the same order, the vertices are considered to be of the same type. Every vertex in a tiling can be of the same type, or there can be several different types of vertices.

In the case of edge-to-edge tessellations of regular polygons, vertices can be simply specified by the types of regular polygons that meet at them. Integers specify different regular polygons; e.g., an equilateral triangle is specified by the number 3, and a regular hexagon by the number 6. A vertex is then specified by listing the regular polygons meeting at it. For consistency, in the examples below the smallest number is listed first, and remaining ones in order proceeding clockwise around the vertex.

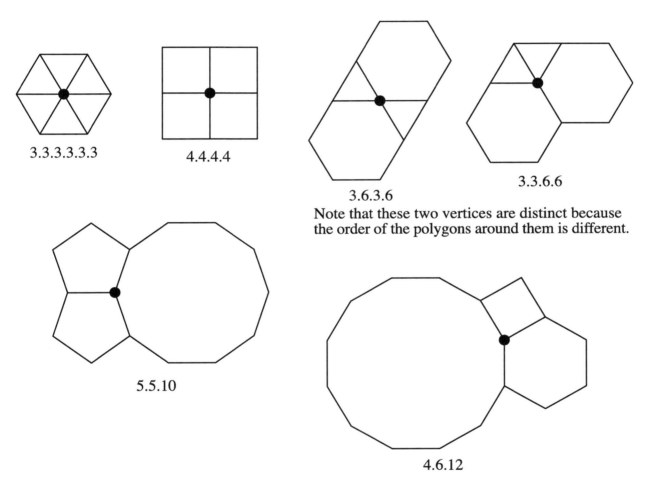

3.3.3.3.3.3

4.4.4.4

3.6.3.6

3.3.6.6

Note that these two vertices are distinct because the order of the polygons around them is different.

5.5.10

4.6.12

It can be shown that there are exactly 21 distinct types of vertices that can be formed by arranging regular polygons around a point. However, for 6 of these, there is no edge-to-edge tessellation by regular polygons that contains even a single vertex of that type. The vertex 5.5.10 shown above is one of these.

Prototiles

A tile to which many or all other tiles in the tessellation are similar (have the same shape) is called a prototile. The regular tessellations all have a single prototile, while the semi-regular tessellations shown on the next page all have more than one prototile.

There are eight semi-regular tessellations – edge-to-edge tessellations for which every tile is a regular polygon, there are at least two different regular polygons, and each vertex is of the same type. These tilings are featured in a Tessellations classroom poster titled *Regular Polygon Tessellations*, as well as in the puzzle *Tessel-gons* (see p. 142).

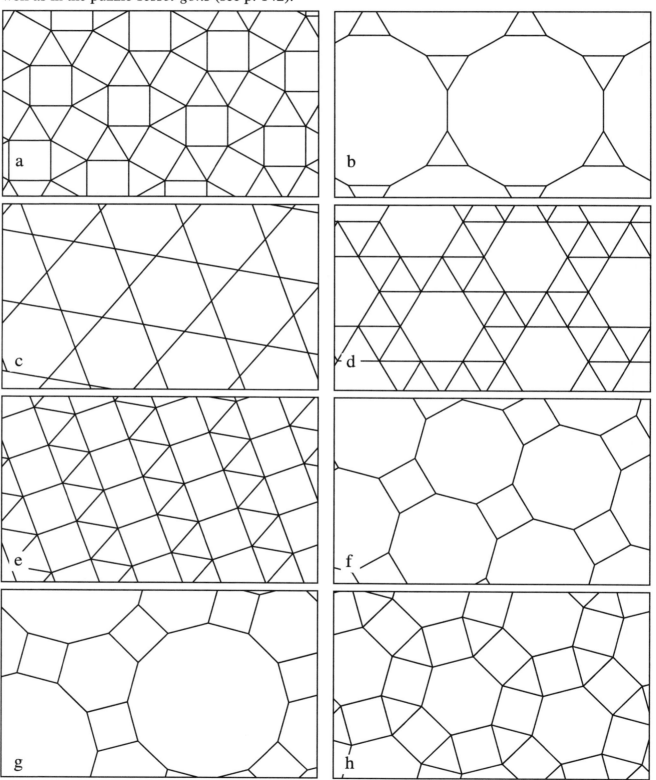

Other Types of Polygons

There are many types of polygons that turn up in tessellations other than regular polygons. Some of these are named and described here. Many of them will be referred to later in the book. Two that are not seen very commonly outside of tessellations are kites and darts.

Isosceles Triangle – One in which two sides are of the same length.

Right Triangle – One that contains a 90° angle.

Rectangle – A quadrilateral in which every angle is 90°. A square is a special case of a rectangle.

Rhombus – A quadrilateral in which every side is of the same length. A square is also a special case of a rhombus.

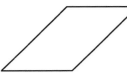

Parallelogram – A quadrilateral in which both pairs of opposing sides are parallel. A rhombus is a special case of a parallelogram.

Trapezoid – A quadrilateral in which one pair of opposing sides are parallel.

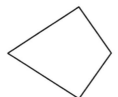

Kite – A quadrilateral with two adjacent sides of one length and two other adjacent sides of a second length, and all angles less than 180°.

Dart – A quadrilateral with two adjacent sides of one length and two other adjacent sides of a second length, and one angle greater than 180°.

All of the polygons above are convex except for the dart. This means that none of their interior angles are greater than 180°. Another type of polygon that has interior angles greater than 180° is star polygons. In these, the angles alternate between convex and concave. Some examples are shown below. Some particular star polygons have names ending with the suffix "gram".

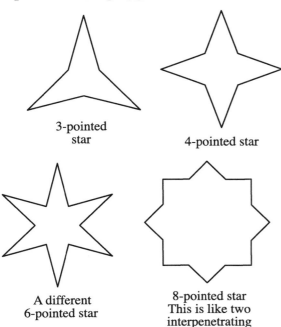

3-pointed star

4-pointed star

5-pointed star (pentagram)

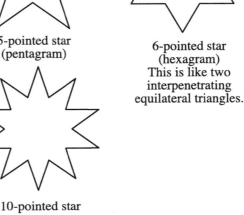

6-pointed star (hexagram) This is like two interpenetrating equilateral triangles.

A different 6-pointed star

8-pointed star This is like two interpenetrating squares.

10-pointed star

General Triangle and Quadrilateral Tessellations

Earlier in the chapter, we saw that equilateral triangles and squares both tessellate. What about triangles that aren't equilateral, and quadrilaterals other than squares? It turns out that any triangle and any quadrilateral will tessellate. Any triangle can be copied, rotated 180°, and joined to an unrotated triangle so that the two form a parallelogram. These parallelograms then tessellate in a straightforward manner.

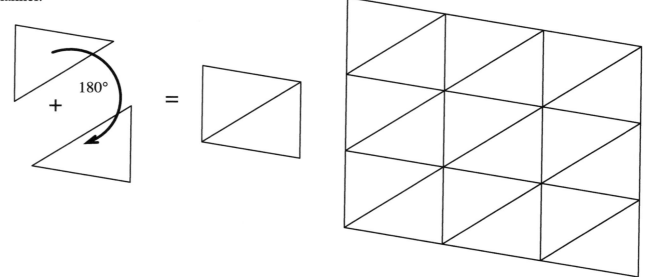

Similarly, any quadrilateral tessellates when paired up with another copy that has been rotated 180°, even if it is concave.

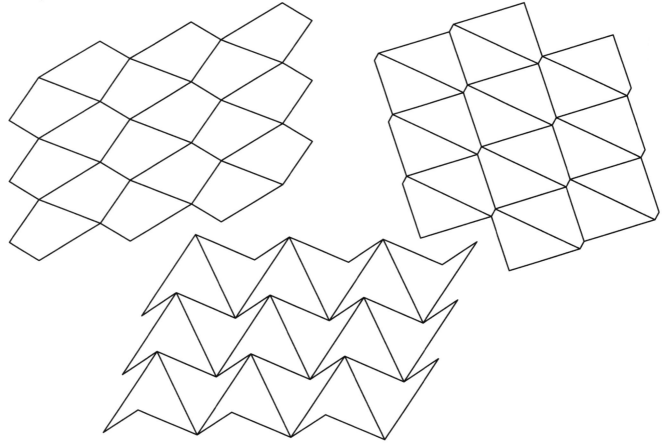

Pentagon and Hexagon Tessellations

Regular pentagons won't tessellate, but there are a variety of other pentagons that will tessellate. There are also many different types of hexagons that will tessellate. Some examples are shown below. Any geometric tessellation can serve as a starting point for creating a tessellation with lifelike motifs.

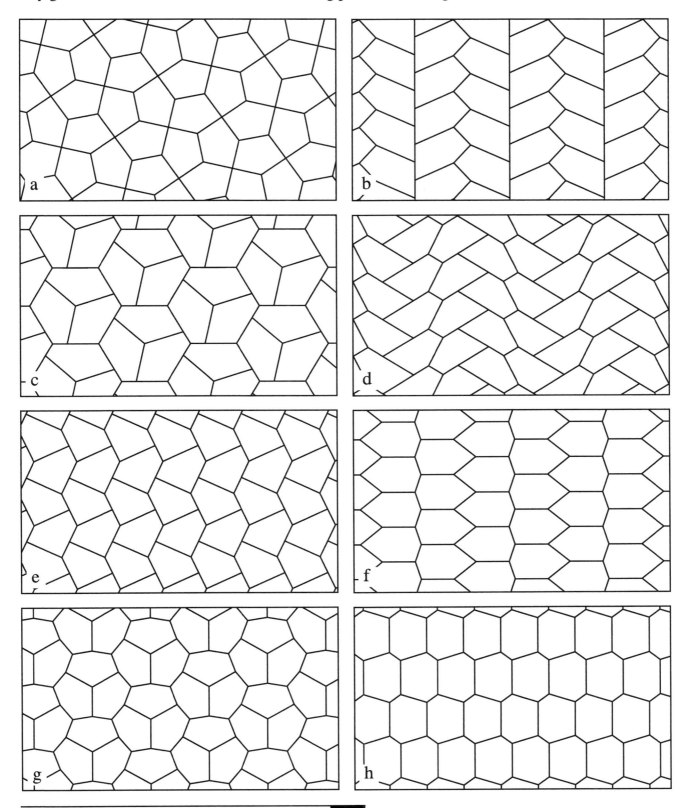

Star Polygon Tessellations

In conjunction with regular polygons, star polygons form a variety of beautiful tessellations. Some examples are given below. These tilings are featured in a Tessellations puzzle called *Tessel-gon Stars* (see p. 142).

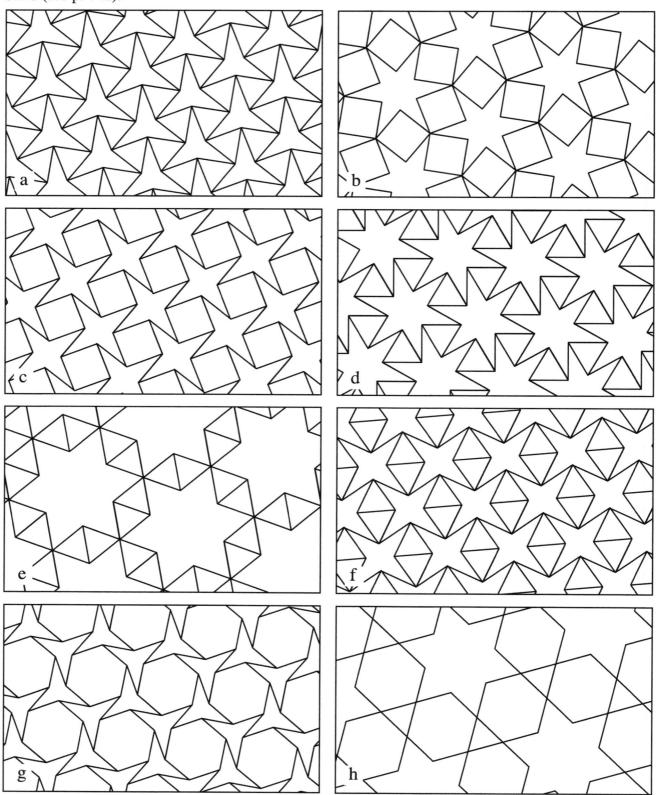

Activities
Activity 3-1. Basic properties of tiles

Materials: Copies of Worksheet 3-1.

Objective: Learn to identify tiles and their edges and corners.

Vocabulary: Tile, polygonal tile, edge, corner.

Activity Sequence:
1. Write the vocabulary terms on the board and discuss the meaning of each one.
2. Pass out copies of the worksheet.
3. For each shape, have the students circle those that are tiles and X through those that aren't.
4. For the polygonal tiles, have the students put a C by each corner and an E by each edge.

Discussion Questions:
1. Is shapes a/b/c/d/e/f/g/h a tile or not?
2. Why or why not?

Activity 3-2. Edge-to-edge tessellations

Materials: Copies of pentagons and hexagons tilings page.

Objective: Learn to identify edge-to-edge tessellations.

Vocabulary: Edge-to-edge tessellation, vertex.

Activity Sequence:
1. Write the vocabulary terms on the board and discuss the meaning of each one.
2. Pass out copies of the pentagons and hexagons tessellations page (p. 27).
3. Have the students write an E in the margin beside each tessellation that is edge-to-edge.
4. Have the students circle one of each distinct vertex in each tessellation and number the distinct types V_1, V_2, etc.

Discussion Questions:
1. Is tessellation a/b/c/d/e/f/g/h edge-to-edge or not?
2. Why or why not?
3. How many distinct types of vertices does tessellation a/b/c/d/e/f/g/h possess? Describe them.

Worksheet 3-1. Basic properties of tiles

For each shape, circle those that are tiles and X through those that aren't.
For those that are, put a C by each corner and an E by each edge.

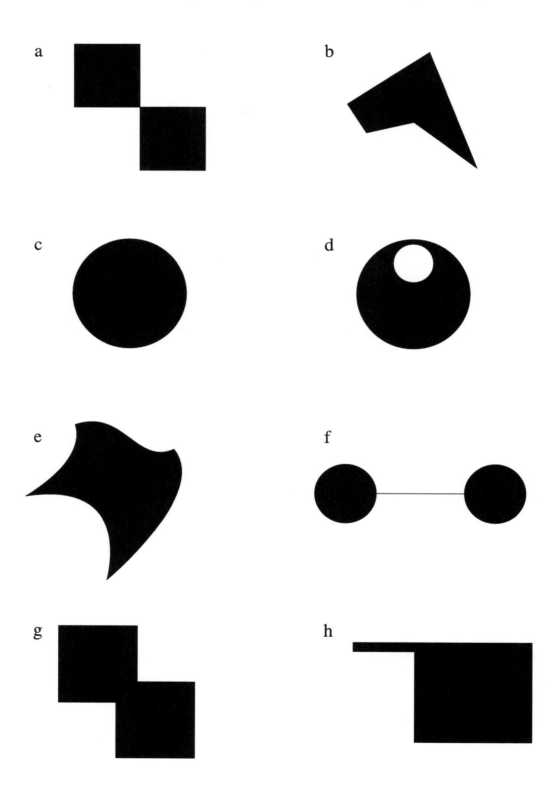

Activity 3-3. Classifying tessellations by their vertices

Materials: Copies of Worksheet 3-3.

Objective: Learn to label vertex types and use those labels to classify tessellations.

Vocabulary: Regular polygon, regular tessellation, semi-regular tessellation.

Activity Sequence:
1. Write the vocabulary terms on the board and discuss the meaning of each one.
2. Pass out copies of the worksheet.
3. Have the students label each tessellation with a label that describes the vertex type.
4. Have them try to draw the tessellation described by the label at bottom right.

Discussion Questions:
1. What is the label for tessellation b/c/d/e/f?
2. Why?
Have a student draw his or her tessellation described by (3.6.3.6) on the board.
3. Is this tessellation consistent with the label (3.6.3.6)? Why or why not?
4. Did anyone draw a different tessellation? Is so, would you like to draw it on the board? Is it consistent with the label (3.6.3.6)?
5. How many different tessellations are there that are consistent with this label?

Worksheet 3-3. Classifying tessellations by their vertices

For each of these regular or semiregular tessellations, write a label that describes the vertex type, as shown in the example. At the bottom right, try to draw the tessellation described by the label.

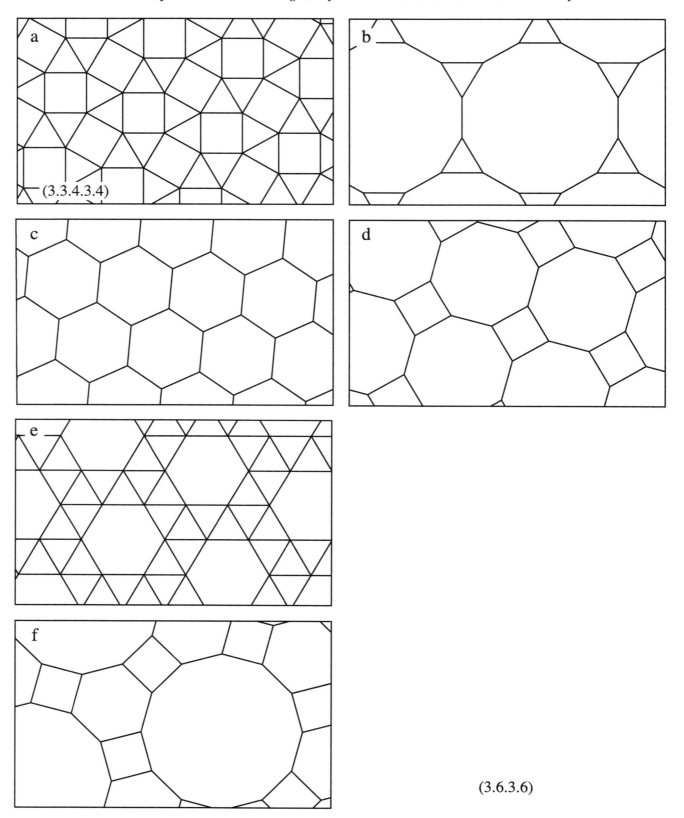

a (3.3.4.3.4)

b

c

d

e

f

(3.6.3.6)

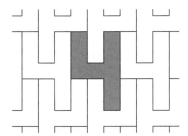

Symmetry and Transformations in Tessellations

Symmetry and transformations are at the heart of what makes tessellations possible. Fortunately, it doesn't require a lot of mathematics background to gain a basic understanding of them. A transformation is an act of moving or changing one thing into another. Symmetry is the property of invariance under a transformation; i.e., not being altered by the transformation.

This chapter covers symmetry in natural and manmade objects, followed by the transformations that make it possible to create Eschersque tiles. Symmetry in tessellations is then described, followed by a brief description of some classification systems for the symmetry of tessellations. Finally, a few comments are made about the coloring of tessellations and how it relates to symmetry.

A classroom poster titled *Symmetry in Tessellations* is available that provides examples of different types of symmetry in Escheresque tessellations (see p. 142).

Mirror Symmetry in Objects

Strictly speaking, an isolated object can only possess two basic types of symmetry – mirror (reflection) and rotational. An object possesses mirror symmetry if it can be reflected about some line (in two dimensions; plane in three dimensions) passing through its center and remain unchanged. An object can possess multiple lines of mirror symmetry. A particular type of mirror symmetry is bilateral symmetry, which means that an object has a single line of mirror symmetry. Most animals have approximate bilateral symmetry when viewed from the front/back or top/bottom.

Real-world objects are never mathematically exact, so it should be understood when referring to symmetry in real objects that it such symmetry is approximate. This is especially true of objects occurring in nature.

All three of these objects possess bilateral symmetry.

Rotational Symmetry in Objects

An object possesses rotational symmetry if it can be rotated by some fraction of a full revolution about its center and remain unchanged. If that fraction is $1/n$ of a full revolution, that object is said to possess n-fold rotational symmetry. An object can possess both reflection and rotational symmetry.

This flower also has 5-fold rotational symmetry, but no lines of mirror symmetry.

This sea star has 5-fold rotational symmetry, as shown, as well as mirror symmetry about five different lines, one of which is indicated.

This wheel possesses mirror symmetry about the line shown, but does not possess rotational symmetry. The 9 spokes alone and the 5 bolts alone possess rotational symmetry, but the wheel as a whole does not.

Translational Symmetry in Objects

An object possesses translational symmetry if it can be translated (moved by some amount in some direction) and remain unchanged. Strictly speaking, a physical object cannot possess translational symmetry, because physical objects are finite in extent. A translation would therefore move part of the object off its original footprint. However, over a limited region, an object can possess translational symmetry. This sort of local translational symmetry is not uncommon.

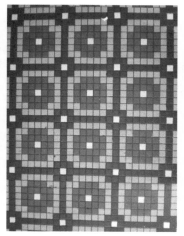

These objects possess local translational symmetry. The window and tiles exhibit local translational symmetry in two dimensions, while the cactus exhibits local translational symmetry in one dimension (vertically).

Glide Reflection Symmetry in Objects

An object possesses glide reflection symmetry if it can be translated along some line (glide) and then be reflected about that line and remain unchanged. Strictly speaking, a physical object cannot possess glide reflection symmetry, because a translation would move part of the object off its original footprint. However, within a limited region, an object can possess glide reflection symmetry.

Both these objects possess local glide reflection symmetry.

Transformations: Translation and Vectors

There are four types of transformations a two-dimensional figure can make within the plane that might leave it unchanged. These are translation, rotation, reflection, and glide reflection. Reflection can be considered a special case of glide reflection in which the glide distance is zero, but the two have traditionally been treated separately by mathematicians.

The simplest transformation is translation, sometimes called a slide or a glide, which is simply movement from one location to another with no rotation or reflection. If an object such as a polygon translates, both a distance and a direction are associated with that movement. This can be indicated with an arrow, as shown below. Such an arrow, indicating both distance and direction is called a vector.

The translation of an object is described by a vector, an arrow indicating both direction and distance.

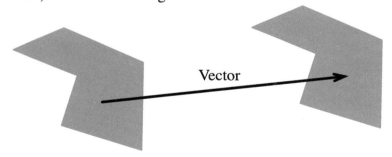

Vector

Two edges of a tile can be related to each other by a translation. In the templates later in this book, this transformation is indicated by an arrow of the sort shown at right. This arrow simply indicates the type of transformation and its direction, not the precise distance. The two solid lines at right are related by a translation that transforms Edge 1 into Edge 2.

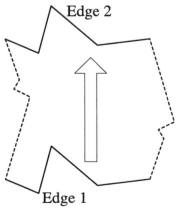

Edge 2

Edge 1

Transformations: Rotation

When an object moves within the plane by rotating without translating or reflecting, that movement can be fully specified by a center of rotation and an angle of rotation between 0 and 360°. For example, the polygon at right has rotated 70° about the point P.

In the templates later in this book, two edges of a tile are often related to each other by a rotation. This is indicated with a curved arrow of the sort shown here.

The two solid edges are related by a rotation of 60° about the vertex V. Edge 1 is transformed into Edge 2 by this rotation.

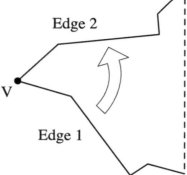

Transformations: Reflection

A reflection is specified simply by a line of mirror symmetry.

In the templates later in this book, if two edges of a tile are related by reflection, the axis of reflection is indicated by a dashed line, with an arrow illustrating the transformation between the two edges. In the example at right, Edge 1 is transformed into Edge 2 by reflection about the axis of reflection indicated. Imagine the arrow forming a sort of bridge above the axis of reflection.

Transformations: Glide Reflection

A glide reflection involves two motions, a translation (or glide) and a reflection.

In the templates later in this book, an arrow twisted 180° is used to indicate a glide reflection transformation between the edges at either end of the arrow, as shown at right. Edge 1 is transformed into Edge 2 by the combination of a glide and a reflection.

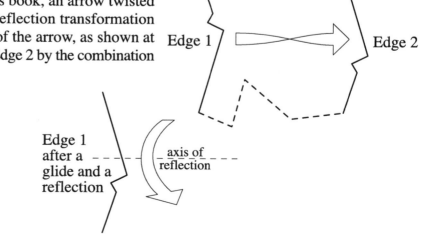

Symmetry in Tessellations: Translation

A tessellation is said to possess translational symmetry if the entire tessellation can be translated (moved by some amount in some direction) and remain unchanged (perfectly overlie itself). A tessellation that possesses translational symmetry is said to be periodic. The translation vector for an infinite tessellation is not unique. In the examples below, the first with a single prototile and the second with four different prototiles, a few different translation vectors are shown that will leave the tessellations unchanged. A puzzle called *In the Garden*, based on the bottom design, is available (see p. 142).

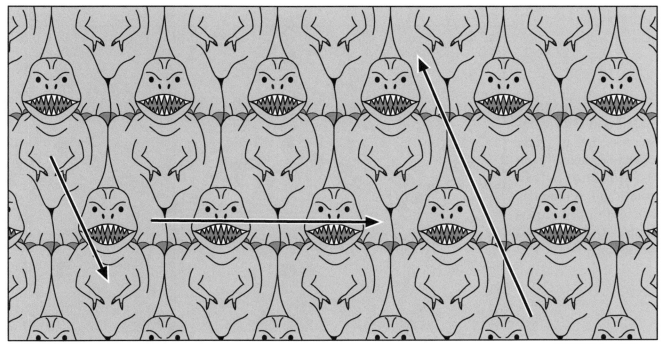

© 2006 Robert Fathauer

© 1996 Robert Fathauer

A tessellation is said to possess *n*-fold rotational symmetry about a point (where *n* is an integer) if the entire tessellation can be rotated by $1/n$ of a full revolution about that point and remain unchanged. The smallest rotation amount should be specified. I.e., if a tessellation possesses 6-fold rotational symmetry, it also possesses 3-fold and 2-fold, but it is referred to as 6-fold. A polygon can be used both to indicate a point of rotational symmetry and to specify the amount of rotation. For example, a rectangle is used to indicate a point of 2-fold rotational symmetry, an equilateral triangle 3-fold, a square 4-fold, a pentagon 5-fold, and so on.

The horned lizard and Gila monster tessellation at right contains points of both 3-fold and 6-fold rotational symmetry, indicated by equilateral triangles and hexagons.

© 1994 Robert Fathauer

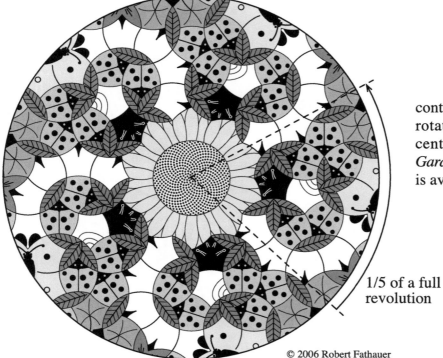

The tessellation at left contains a single point of 5-fold rotational symmetry about its center. A puzzle called *In the Garden Too*, based on this design, is available (see p. 142).

1/5 of a full revolution

© 2006 Robert Fathauer

Symmetry in Tessellations: Glide Reflection

A tessellation is said to possess glide reflection symmetry if the entire tessellation can be translated along some line and then reflected about that line and remain unchanged. Mirror symmetry is a special case of glide reflection symmetry in which the glide distance is zero, and it is not treated separately here as a symmetry of tessellations. The first tessellation below possesses mirror symmetry about each of the long-dashed lines. Ignoring colors, it also possesses glide reflection symmetry about the short-dashed lines. The second tessellation below possesses two distinct lines of glide reflection symmetry, as indicated by dashed lines. A couple of possible glide vectors are indicated. In both cases, the full tessellation possesses infinitely many lines of each type.

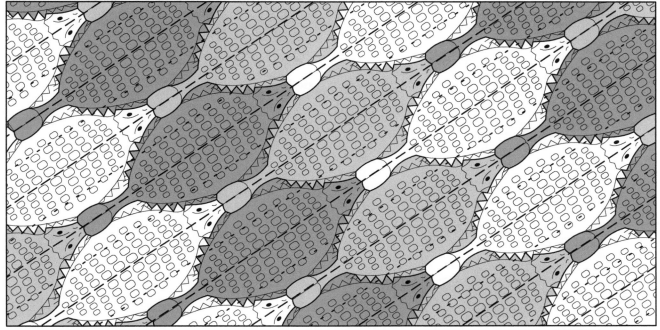

© 2005 Robert Fathauer

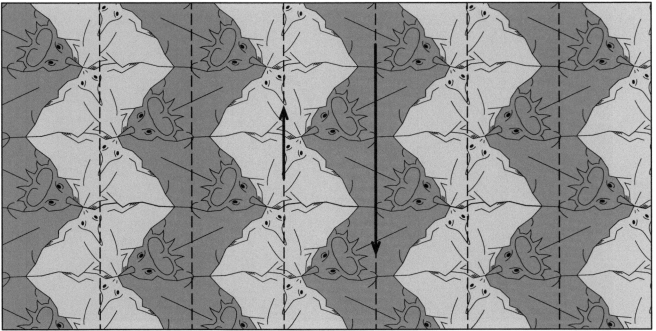

© 2005 Robert Fathauer

Unit Cells

A unit cell is the smallest group of tiles that may be copied repeatedly and used to generate the entire tessellation through translation only. The concept of a unit cell only makes sense for tessellations that possess translational symmetry. The exact choice of unit cell is not unique, as shown below by the two groups with heavy outline, but each choice of unit cell will contain the same number and types of the tiles, in the same orientations. A puzzle called *Squids & Rays*, based on this design but without the sea turtles, is available (see p. 142).

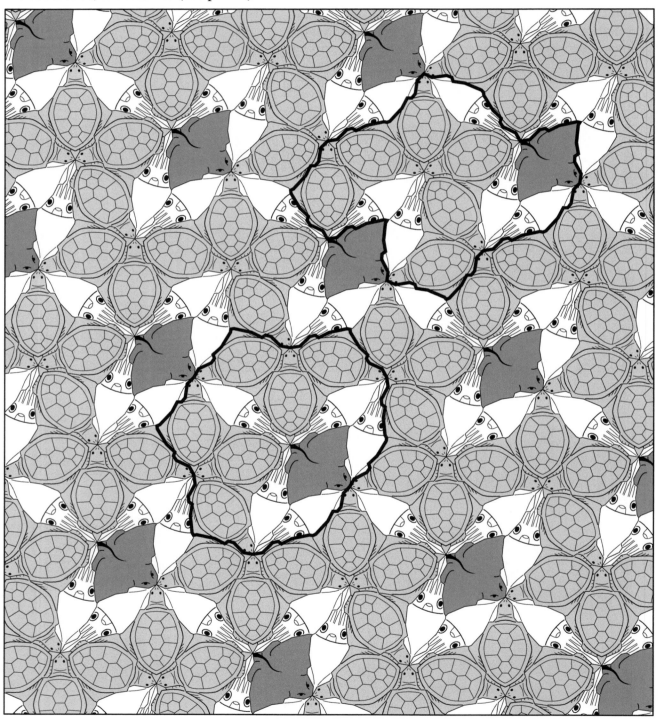

Symmetry Groups and Heesch Types

There are several different classification systems used for patterns and tessellations. Two of the most useful for Escheresque tessellations are the plane symmetry group and the Heesch type.

There are 17 plane symmetry groups, also known as wallpaper groups, into which all periodic two-dimensional patterns and tessellations fall. These are the collections of translations, rotations, reflections, and glide reflections that leave a design unchanged. For each of the templates provided in later chapters, the symmetry group is given. Examples of symmetry group notation are *p3*, *p4g*, and *cmm*. The leading *p* or *c* stand for primitive cell or face-centered cell; this has to do with whether or not the region of the pattern used to describe the symmetries has internal repetition. If there is a number in the second position, it indicates the highest order of rotational symmetry. The subsequent *m*, *g*, or *1* (there can be more than one *m* or *g* for different axes) indicate mirror, glide reflection, or neither.

Heinrich Heesch classified all of the distinct types of asymmetric tiles that will tessellate. He found 28 distinct types in the early 1930's, but didn't publish these results until 1963. By this time, M.C. Escher had already worked out his own classification system, which included almost all of the Heesch types. Escher's system has some similarities to Heesch's, but is harder to understand, so it won't be described here. For each of the templates provided in later chapters, the Heesch type is given when applicable. For designing Escheresque tiles, mirror symmetry is often useful, since many living creative have bilateral symmetry. Tiles of this sort are excluded from Heesch's classification, since they are not asymmetric. In addition, Heesch's system only includes tessellations with a single prototile. In contrast, a symmetry group can be assigned to every tessellation.

Heesch's notation is simple and not difficult to understand. It describes the tile in terms of the transformations relating its edges. The letter T denotes translation, G glide reflection, and C rotation. A translation must always be from one side of the tile to the opposing side, so subscripts are not needed for T. For G, there is no subscript if there is only one line that is transformed by glide reflection, and subscripts 1 and 2 to differentiate when there are two lines of glide reflection. For C, the subscript indicates the amount of rotation. C without a subscript indicates 1/2 of a full revolution, 3 indicates 1/3, 4 indicates 1/4, and 6 indicates 1/6.

To use Heesch's system, first label each edge of a tile. The edges are always labeled in pairs except for edges with 2-fold rotational symmetry. Once the edges are labeled, the tile is described by going around it in a circuit, listing the edge types. Some examples are shown below, with vertices indicated by dots (one needs to see the tessellation to see where the vertices are). At left, the tile has four edges, with opposing sides related by translation. Each edge is labeled T, and the Heesch type is simply TTTT. At middle, two of the three edges are related by a glide reflection, while the third edge possesses 2-fold rotational symmetry bout the tick mark. The labels are then G, G, and C, and the Heesch type is CGG. In the right example, the six sides occur in pairs that are related by rotations of 1/3 of a full revolution. Thus each side is labeled C_3, and the Heesch type is $C_3C_3C_3C_3C_3C_3$.

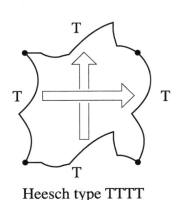

Heesch type TTTT

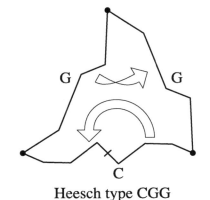

Heesch type CGG

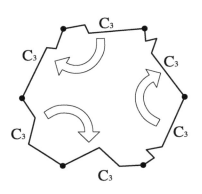

Heesch type $C_3C_3C_3C_3C_3C_3$

Coloring of Tessellations and Symmetry

There are many ways to color a tessellation. In most cases, adjacent tiles are given different colors so they visually stand out more. Escher obeyed this rule in all of his tessellations. A mathematical question here is the minimum number of colors required to accomplish this for a given tessellation. All tessellations that are Heesch types require either two or three colors.

Another choice is to color all tiles of a given type the same, regardless of whether or not they are adjacent. An example of this is the squids, rays, and sea turtles tessellation earlier in this chapter.

Symmetry is one concern in the choice of the coloring of tessellations. A given coloring can preserve all, some, or none of the symmetries of a tessellation. For example, if a particular glide reflection leaves an uncolored tessellation unchanged, does it still leave the colored tessellation unchanged? Visually, a choice that preserves symmetries will bring out the mathematical symmetry more.

A particular type of coloring Escher considered is perfect coloring. In a perfectly-colored tessellation, it isn't necessarily the case that a symmetry operation that leaves an uncolored tessellation unchanged will leave the colored tessellation unchanged. However, any changes must take the form of an unambiguous permutation (swapping out) of the colors. For example, if a tessellation has red, green, and blue tiles, a symmetry operation that moves a blue tile onto a red tile must move every blue tile onto a red tile. In a perfectly colored tessellation, symmetries that permute the colors, as opposed to leaving them unchanged, are called color symmetries. These are color-exchanging symmetries of the design. A mathematical question here is the minimum number of colors required to perfectly color a tessellation. This number can be greater than the minimum number required to prevent adjacent tiles having the same color.

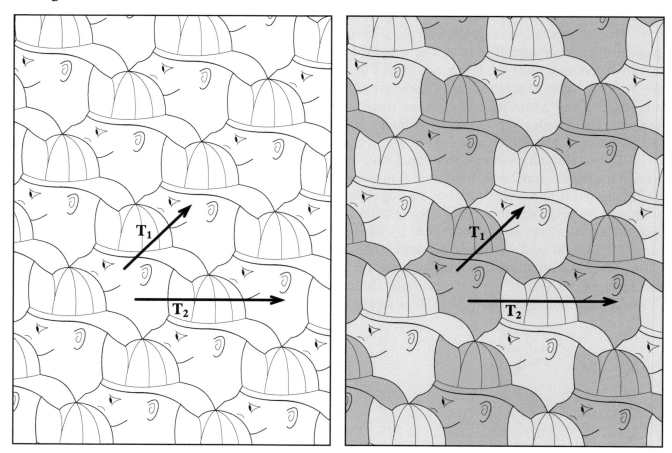

Translation T_1 doesn't change the uncolored tessellation, but does change the colored one. However, every light tile is made dark, and every dark tile is made light. Translation T_2 changes neither the uncolored nor colored tessellations. Since any other translation would be equivalent to one of these two, the coloring is perfect.

Activities

Activity 4-1. Symmetry in Objects

Materials: Copies of Worksheet 4-1.

Objective: Learn to identify rotational and mirror symmetry in manmade and natural objects.

Vocabulary: Rotational symmetry, mirror symmetry, bilateral symmetry.

Activity Sequence:
1. Write the vocabulary words on the board and discuss the meaning of each.
2. Pass out copies of the worksheet.
3. First go over the example. Then have students mark the lines of mirror symmetries and write down the rotational symmetry of the objects on the page.

Discussion Questions:
1. How many lines of symmetry did you mark for object a/b/c/d/e/f/g? Why?
2. Does object a/b/c/d/e/f/g possess rotational symmetry? If so, what is the minimum rotation n that will leave the object unchanged?

Activity 4-2. Transformations

Materials: Copies of Worksheet 4-2.

Objective: Learn to identify transformations in Eschersque tiles.

Vocabulary: Translation, rotation, glide reflection.

Activity Sequence:
1. Write the vocabulary words on the board and discuss the meaning of each.
2. Pass out copies of the worksheet.
3. First go over the example. Then have students mark and label the transformations between the two edges marked "a" for each tile.

Discussion Questions:
1. What sort of transformation did you mark for tile a/b/c/d/e/f? Why?

Activity 4-3. Translational symmetry in tessellations

Materials: Copies of the Star Polygon Tessellations page (p. 28) from Chapter 3.

Objective: Learn to identify translational symmetry in tessellations, and to mark unit cells and translation vectors.

Vocabulary: Translational symmetry, vector, unit cell.

Activity Sequence:
1. Write the vocabulary words on the board and discuss the meaning of each.
2. Pass out copies of the star polygon tessellations, page 28.

3. For each tessellation, have the students draw two different translation vectors that would leave the tessellation unchanged.
4. For each tessellation, have the students outline the unit cell.

Discussion Questions:
1. Share a vector you drew for tessellation a/b/c/d/e/f/g/h.
2. Does anyone think the vector shown is not a translation vector for this tessellation? If so, why?
3. How many tiles of each type are contained in the unit cell for tessellation a/b/c/d/e/f/g/h?
4. Did anyone get a different result? If so, which is correct, and why?

Activity 4-4. Rotational symmetry in tessellations

Materials: Copies of the Semi-regular Tessellations page (p. 24) from Chapter 3.

Objective: Learn to identify rotational symmetry in tessellations, and to mark rotation points with polygons indicating the amount of rotation.

Vocabulary: Rotational symmetry.

Activity Sequence:
1. Write the vocabulary term on the board and discuss its meaning.
2. Pass out copies of the semi-regular tessellations, page 24.
3. For each tessellation, have the students draw a polygon on each distinct point of rotational symmetry. Have them use a rectangle for points of 2-fold rotational symmetry, a triangle for 3-fold, a square for 4-fold, and a hexagon for 6-fold.

Discussion Questions:
1. Share your polygon locations and types for tessellation a/b/c/d/e/e/f/g/h.
2. Does anyone think any of the polygons are not the right type or at the right location? Why?
3. Did anyone find any additional distinct points of rotational symmetry for the tessellation?

Activity 4-5. Glide reflection symmetry in tessellations

Materials: Copies of the Pentagon and Hexagon Tessellations page (p. 27) from Chapter 3.

Objective: Learn to identify glide reflection symmetry in tessellations, and to mark glide lines and vectors.

Vocabulary: Mirror symmetry, glide reflection symmetry, vector.

1. Write the vocabulary terms on the board and discuss their meanings.
2. Pass out copies of the pentagon and hexagon tessellations, page 27.
3. For each tessellation, have the students mark lines of mirror and glide reflection symmetry, labeling the former "M", the latter "G", and indicating a possible glide vector for the latter.

Discussion Questions:
1. Do any of the tessellations possess neither mirror nor glide reflection symmetry? Which one(s)?
2. Do any of the tessellations possess both mirror and glide reflection symmetry? Which one(s)?
3. How many distinct lines of glide reflection symmetry does tessellation a/b/c/d/e/f/g/h possess?

Worksheet 4-1. Identifying symmetry in objects

Mark the lines of mirror symmetries and write down the rotational symmetry of the objects on this page, as shown for the example. If the object does not possess rotational symmetry, write "No rotational symmetry".

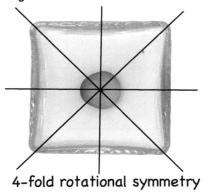

4-fold rotational symmetry

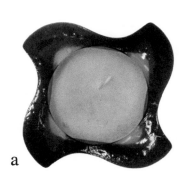

a

b

c

d

e

f

g

Worksheet 4-2. Identifying transformations

*For each tile below, use arrows to indicate the transformation that relates the two edges marked "a",
and write the type of transformation, as shown in the examples.*

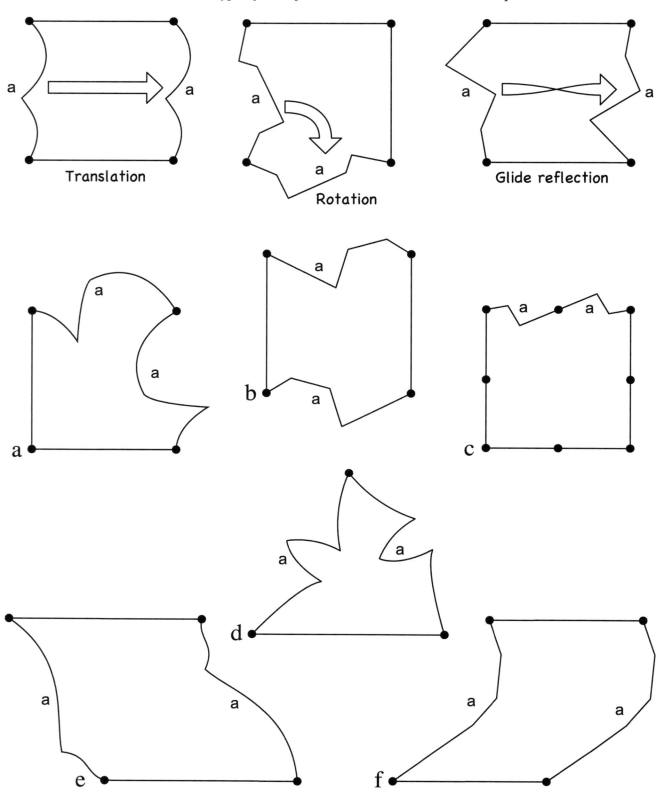

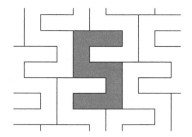

Tips on Designing and Drawing Escheresque Tessellations

Creating an Escheresque tessellation can be divided into two main tasks. The first is designing the prototile or prototiles, the tile or tiles to which all of the tiles in the tessellation are similar. The second is making multiple copies of the prototile(s) to form the full tessellation. The second task is relatively straightforward once you understand the mathematical rules for creating a particular tessellation. The following chapters provide numerous templates, as well as grids, to help you create tessellations. These templates describe exactly how the rules work for a wide variety of tessellations. A detailed example is described in Chapter 7, walking you through each step in the process.

The first task, designing your prototile(s), is probably the more challenging part of making a good tessellation. It involves a lot of creativity, as well as patience and perseverance. The task of designing your prototile(s) has two facets, designing the outline of the tile(s) and drawing the internal details. These two tasks go hand-in-hand when creating a prototile. You will probably find yourself going back and forth between the two as you refine your design.

The first step in designing your prototile is to distort the edges of the tile. You need to exercise your creativity to recognize a motif emerging from a tile that you're distorting. You then guide further distortions to make the tile to look more like that motif. In a tessellation, every line segment is shared by two tiles. This means that changing a line to make a tile look better in one area could make another portion of the tile (or of a second tile) look worse.

Designing an Escheresque tile is easier if you choose motifs that are flexible. Some animals can be twisted around and distorted quite a bit, while other can't be. Lizards, birds, and fish seem to work particularly well, and M.C. Escher used these motifs for many of his tessellations. As a motif, people are especially challenging. Not only are they not very flexible, but the human eye is more sensitive to whether or not people look right than to whether or not other animals that we don't see as often look right.

The purpose of this chapter and the next is to provide guidelines and tips to help you create the best possible prototile(s) and tessellations. The first four tips in this chapter lay out goals to strive for in order to realize an effective tessellation. Achieving all of these design goals in the same tessellation is often not possible, and you'll notice that many of the tessellations in this book fall short of these ideals. Tips 5-8 provide ways to improve your designs. Chapter 6 describes special tricks and techniques to help you solve problems or further improve your designs.

Hand and Computer Approaches to Drawing Tessellations

Some people create tessellations completely by hand, some completely by computer, and some using a mixture of the two. How you choose to work depends on your background, skills, and personal preferences. Different approaches are compared and contrasted below.

Working by Hand

It is entirely possible to create unique and beautiful tessellations without the use of computers. M.C. Escher worked this way, and some people still prefer to do so today. However, Escher was a graphic artist by training, and computer graphics were virtually non-existent until late in his life. On the positive side, working by hand frees you up to draw in a more relaxed and spontaneous fashion. This may help you to be more creative. A hand drawn and colored tessellation may look more artistic than one created by computer, as these hand techniques are the traditional means of creating art. On the negative side, it is difficult to accurately draw the same lines over and over again, particularly when they are reflected. It can also be tedious to repeatedly draw the same features in order to tessellate a large area such as a full sheet of paper. If your drawing skills are not very developed, it takes even longer and can be more difficult to achieve satisfactory results working by hand.

Using General Computer Graphics Programs

Tiles can be created using drawing programs that are not specifically designed for tessellations. These programs allow easy duplicating, rotating, translating, and reflecting of lines and other elements. All of the templates in the later chapter can easily be set up using such a program. While it is more difficult to draw interior details using a computer, they only need to be drawn once, after which the entire tile with interior details can be duplicated and transformed to create a larger tessellation. This is how I personally create tessellations, using the program FreeHand. Other popular program of this sort include Illustrator and CorelDRAW. Sometimes, after I have created a tessellation using FreeHand, I will copy tiles and paste them into PhotoShop to perform additional rendering for a final artwork.

Using a Tessellations Computer Program

Computer programs have been written specifically for creating tessellations. An early program that has been used in many classrooms is *TesselMania!*, by Kevin Lee. A more recent program by Kevin is *Tessellation Exploration*. It is easier to create a tessellating tile using these programs, which automate the duplicating, rotating, and other operations. They are also helpful in visualizing and understanding transformations. They provide easy coloring of tiles, and also drag-and-drop interior features like eyes. I personally find these programs limiting, however, so I have not used them for creating my own tessellations. They have a limited number of templates and limited control over the shaping of lines. They don't allow the same degree of polish and control over the appearance of the final tessellation that a full-featured drawing program allows.

Mixing Techniques

The above approaches can be combined, of course. You might want to use a tessellation program to design your tile shape, and then create a final version using other software. Or you might design your tile shape using a drawing program, and then print the outlines of the shapes and draw the interior details by hand. You might create both the tile shape and interior details using a computer, and then just do the coloring by hand. You should try different approaches and decide what works best for you.

Tip 1: To the extent possible, the outline of the tile should suggest the motif even without interior details.

It's often possible to make a shape that doesn't particularly look like a lifelike motif and make it take on life with the interior details. While this sort of tessellation can be effective, it's more satisfying if the shape by itself conjures up a motif. In the examples below, most people wouldn't think T-Rex if they saw the left shape by itself. On the other hand, a winged dragon or something similar is immediately suggested by the right shape. It usually takes more work to create a shape like that on the right, but the resulting tessellation is more compelling because the individual tiles are more interesting. You might want to look at some of Escher's tessellations to see which ones have outlines that suggest the motif and which ones need the interior details to guide your interpretation of the tile(s).

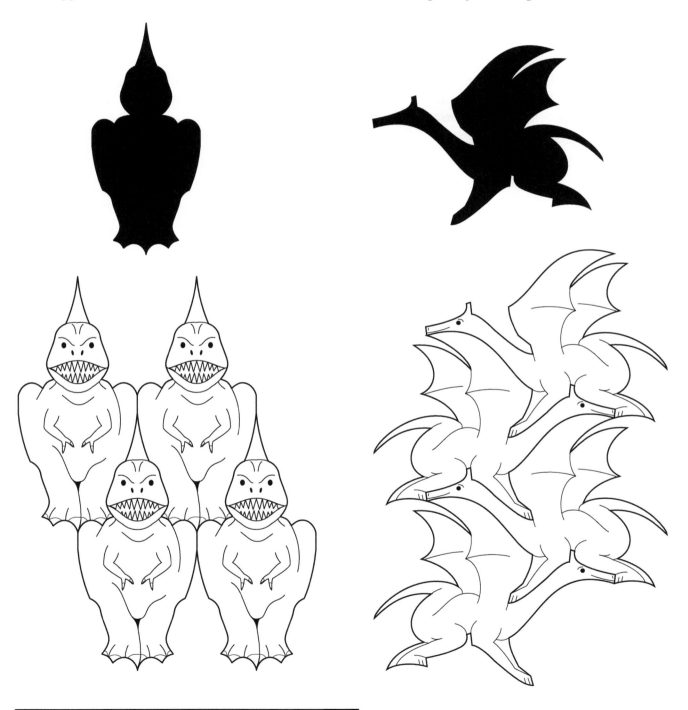

Tip 2: The tiles should make orientational sense.

In a tessellation, like most artwork, you are creating a scene and to a degree telling a story. That scene will look more natural if the motifs are oriented in a way that is consistent with the world around us. Most of the time, your motifs will either be drawn from a top view or a side view. Whichever it is, the two shouldn't be mixed unless you're trying to achieve a special effect. If you're using a side view, then you usually will want the ground at the bottom and the sky at the top, even if these are only implied, not actually shown. Another way of stating this is to say that gravity should be pulling all of the tiles in the same direction.

The example below shows two tessellations of rays. In the left version, each tile is identical. As a result, half the rays are swimming right-side up, and half upside down. In the right version, the shapes of half the tiles have been modified slightly and the interior details changed, so that all of the rays are swimming right-side up. This makes for a more effective design.

As you design a tessellation with a side-view perspective, you may need to reorient your entire tessellation, rotating the paper or rotating all of the tiles on your computer screen, in order to get the pull of gravity in the downward direction. If you look at Escher's tessellations, you'll find that almost all of them make orientational sense, other than his very earliest attempts.

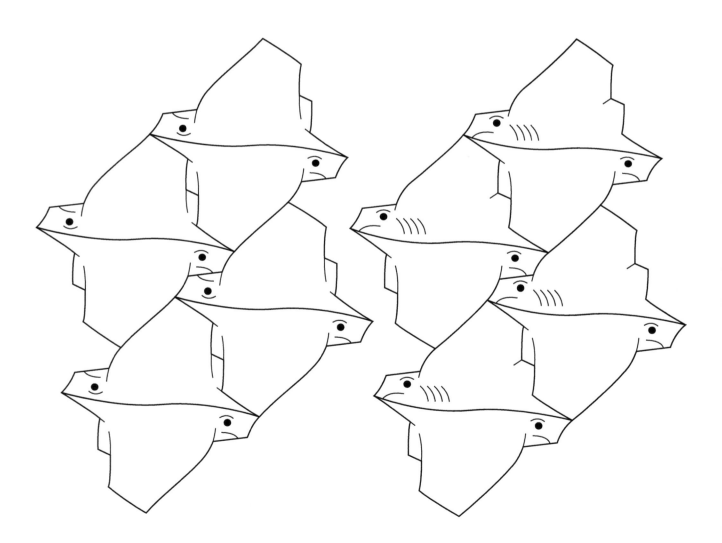

Tip 3: When using more than one motif, choose motifs that go together.

A tessellation makes more sense, in effect tells a better story, if all of the motifs go together. They can be either similar or contrasting. The example below has three similar motifs – beetles, moths, and bumblebees, all three of which are insects. Note that they are all seen from a top view, so the tessellation also makes orientational sense. An example of contrasting motifs is angels and devils, used by M.C. Escher in one of most famous prints. Another famous example by Escher is the use of birds and fish, contrasting the elements sky and water. It wouldn't make sense to use motifs that have no clear relationship to each other, such as dinosaurs along with flowers, or boats along with cats. When Escher used boats, he used them with fish, which makes sense as both are found in the sea. The tessellation puzzles I designed combined like motifs: *Squids & Rays*; *Beetles, Moths, & Bumblebees*; *Frogs, Lizards, & Snakes*;*In the Garden*; and *Out in Space* (see p. 142).

Tip 4: The different motifs should be commensurately scaled, unless a special effect is desired.

As is the case with orienting motifs consistently, scaling motifs commensurately makes the scene created by the tessellation more natural. For example, if giraffes and gorillas were used in a tessellation, it would look odd if they were the same height. In the first example at right, three different sea creatures, squids, rays, and sea turtles, are commensurately scaled.

Intentionally using a different scale for different motifs can create a whimsical effect, as shown at the bottom of this page. In this case, the design is more effective if the scales are very different. Note that monkeys with bananas and cats with mice are motifs that are naturally associated with each other.

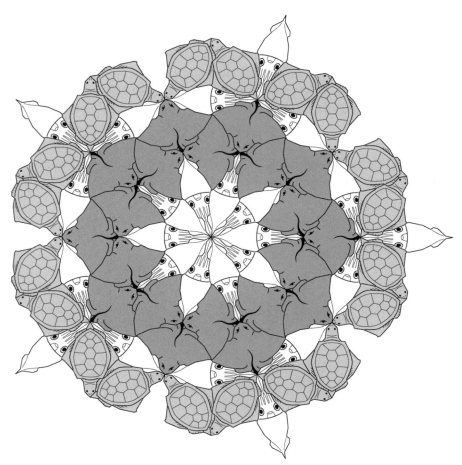

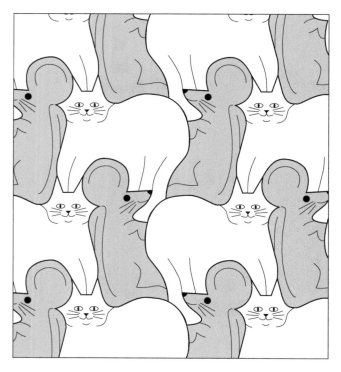

Tip 5: For real world motifs, it is important to use source material to get the details right.

A motif used for a tile can be something imaginary, like a dragon, or it can be something found in the real world. If a real world motif like a lizard, fish, or flower is used, it will look more natural if it is modeled after a specific type of lizard, fish, or flower. Trying to draw motifs from memory is challenging and will probably not yield the best results. Identifying a real-world motif that looks similar to your tile can be very helpful in improving the appearance of the tile. You can find source material like photographs and realistic illustrations in books or the Internet, and these can help guide your design. You may want to place some photos or illustrations right next to your tile as you refine its shape and interior details.

For example, you might decide that your tile will be a fish with its tail folded over, or a flower, or a ray, as shown below. Initial attempts at adding detail may not yield satisfactory results. You might realize it doesn't look right, but not know why. Looking at pictures of different types of fish, you might decide that your shape looks a little like a trout or a bass. You can then search images of these types of fish till you find one or two that you can use as models. You might find that you drew the eye in the wrong place, or a fin is shaped wrong, or the gills can be drawn in to give the head shape. For the flower example, you might decide the petals look similar to those of a daffodil. Even though real daffodils have six petals, using a daffodil-like central structure makes for a reasonably realistic-looking flower. The manta ray provides another example, where the outline was modified slightly to accommodate more realistic anatomical details.

Initial outline:

Initial interior details:

Improved tile based on source material:

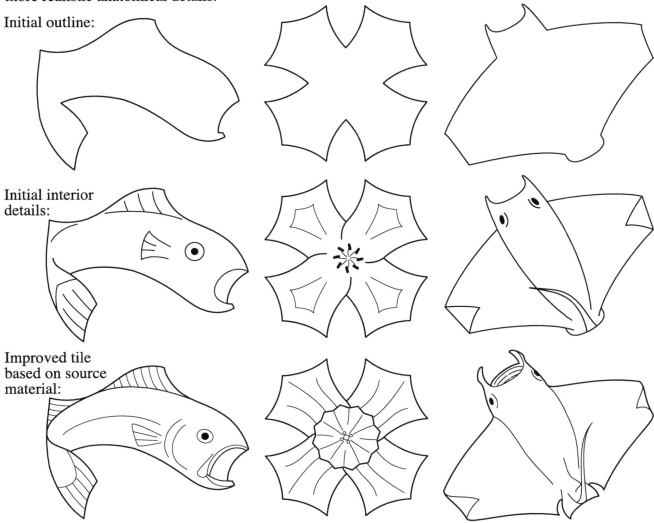

Tip 6: Stylize the design. Don't try to make it look too realistic.

While it is important to get the details right when designing tiles with real-world motifs, trying to include too much detail or trying to make it look too real are generally pitfalls to be avoided. The reason is that the constraints of making tiles fit together without gaps necessitates some distortion of motifs compared to their natural shapes. Trying to make a motif look too realistic tends to make these distortions more obvious. The optimum balance between stylizing a design and making it realistic will depend on how distorted the tile is compared to the real object.

The fact that every line segment is shared by two tiles means that the amount of convex (bulging outward from the center of the tile) and concave (curved inward toward the center of the tile) line segments for a tessellation must be equal. This means that it's impossible to create a tessellation consisting entirely of motifs that are completely made up of convex line segments. Most animals, such as frogs, consist mainly of convex surfaces, though, so a realistic drawing would need mostly convex lines. The drawings below contrast a realistic drawing of frogs with a tessellation of frogs. The feet are particularly challenging, and the sort of wide duck-like foot used here was commonly used by Escher in his frogs and lizards. The more realistic frogs consist almost entirely of convex lines, and it isn't possible to fit them together without gaps.

The cats below provide another example. In this case, the outline of the cat is left rather abstract, consisting of straight-line segments, most of which would be convex curves in a more realistic drawing. Note that there are very few interior details in the bodies, as they would just call attention to the distortion of the outlines.

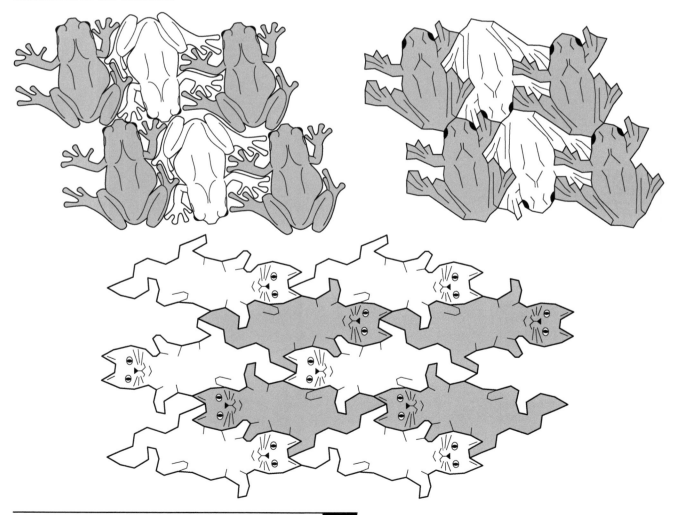

Tip 7: Choose a style that fits your taste and abilities.

There are many choices in drawing style for a tessellation, just like any artwork, but some of these are unique to tessellations. A basic choice discussed earlier in this chapter is whether to work by hand or by computer. Another choice is the degree of realism vs. stylization. For a stylized drawing, there are choices such as serious, cartoon-like, humorous, etc. Within these choices there are subchoices. E.g., if you choose a cartoon-like style, there are many choices within that, from early Disney to contemporary Japanese manga. M.C. Escher's style in some cases tended toward the grotesque. This European style includes fanciful or imagined creatures, so in that sense it lent itself naturally to tessellations.

An aspect of style that is more-or-less unique to tessellations is the use or omission of border lines around tiles. If border lines are used, they can be narrow or wide. M.C. Escher's borders varied from none to very wide.

The same tile is shown below with several different drawing styles. At upper left, the lines are drawn with an ink pen, and the shading done with a colored pencil. At upper right, graphite pencils were used. The next three versions were all done using a computer drawing program, FreeHand. The lower-right example uses photographic rendering, where swatches of a photograph of an actual fish were distorted and blended in PhotoShop to fill the tile boundary.

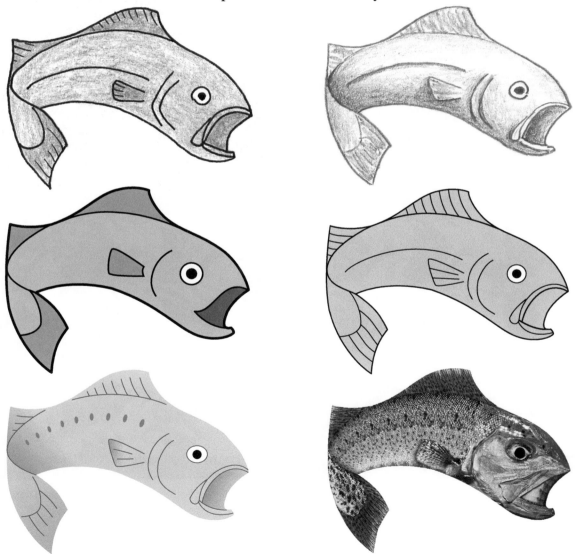

Tip 8: Choose colors that suit your taste and that bring out the tiles.

In a tessellation, it is usually desirable, but not essential, to use different colors for adjacent tiles to provide some contrast. A broad choice of colors is available, as for other types of art. Colors can be bold or subtle, similar or complimentary, warm or cool, etc. You may want to draw from nature; e.g., the undersides of many rays are pale in color, while the tops are dark. Or you may wish to use less naturalistic colors. Each tile can be made essentially one color, or the color can be varied within a tile.

Neighboring tiles can be greatly contrasting in value (lightness or darkness), or similar in value. One choice in a tessellation that lends itself to two colors is to use black for one set of tiles and white for the other tiles. This was used by Escher to achieve a sort of optical illusion in which figure (objects in the foreground) and ground (the background) reverse. The example below illustrates figure/ground reversal in a tessellation of dragons. At the left end, the mind sees black dragons brought forward against a white background, while white dragons are brought forward against a black background at the right end. In the center region, where there is a tessellation of white and black dragons, whether the white dragons or black dragons are seen as being in the foreground depends largely on whether your eye was last on the right or the left edge. As the eye moves back and forth over the drawing, there is a somewhat disconcerting flip between black and white serving as backdrop. Escher used this trick effectively in one of his best known prints, *Day and Night*, which features a tessellation of black and white birds flying over a landscape in which a village is in daylight on one side and darkness on the other.

"Dragons"

Activities

This chapter contains activities that are art oriented, as opposed to earlier chapters, in which the activities were primarily math oriented. Activities in later chapters will contain more of a mixture of art and math.

Activity 5-1. Finding motifs for a tile shape

Materials: Copies of Worksheet 5-1.

Objective: Learn to see motifs in tile shapes and to use interior lines to make the motif more convincing.

Vocabulary: Motif, interior details, orientation, viewpoint.

Activity Sequence:
1. Write the vocabulary terms on the board and discuss the meaning of each.
2. Pass out copies of the worksheet.
3. For each tile, have the students imagine possible motifs by rotating the paper (looking at the tile in different orientations) and considering different viewpoints (e.g., side view or top view). Once they have a motif in mind, they should draw interior details.

Discussion Questions:
1. For tile shape a/b/c/d/e/f/g/h, what motif did you choose?
2. Did anyone choose a different motif? If so, what?
3. For the motif you chose, describe the orientation and viewpoint you chose, and how you used interior details to make it look more like your motif.
4. How well do you think it turned out?
5. What might you have done differently?

Activity 5-2. Refining a tile shape using translation

Materials: Copies of Worksheet 5-2.

Objective: Learn to improve a tessellation that possesses translational symmetry by modifying the edges of the tile.

Vocabulary: Translation.

Activity Sequence:
1. Write the vocabulary term on the board and discuss its meaning.
2. Pass out copies of the worksheet.
3. Have the students reshape the tile as described on the worksheet.

Discussion Questions:
1. How did you reshape line a?
2. Do you think you succeeded in improving your motif? How?
3. How did you reshape line b?
4. Do you think you succeeded in improving your motif? How?

Activity 5-3. Refining a tile shape using glide reflection

Materials: Copies of Worksheet 5-3.

Objective: Learn to improve a tessellation that possesses glide reflection symmetry by modifying the edges of the tile.

Vocabulary: Glide reflection.

Activity Sequence:
1. Write the vocabulary term on the board and discuss its meaning.
2. Pass out copies of the worksheet.
3. Have the students reshape the tile as described on the worksheet.

Discussion Questions:
1. How did you reshape line a?
2. Do you think you succeeded in improving your motif? How?
3. How did you reshape line b? Did you find it difficult to draw two instances of the line, with the second instance mirrored compared to the first?
4. Do you think your modification of line b succeeded in improving your motif? How?

Activity 5-4. Locating and using source material for real-life motifs

Materials: Access to a library or to a computer with Internet access. Copies of Worksheet 5-4.

Objective: Learn to locate source material using books or the Internet, and learn to use it to improve the appearance of the tiles for a tessellation.

Vocabulary: Source material, stylized drawing, realistic drawing.

Activity Sequence:
1. Write the vocabulary terms on the board and discuss their meanings.
2. Pass out copies of the worksheet.
3. Have the students draw interior details in the leftmost outlines provided, working from their mental conception of what each motif should look like.
4. Have the students locate source material for each of the three motifs.
5. Have the students use their source material to draw interior details in the second and third copies of the outlines provided.

Discussion Questions:
1. When you looked at source material, were there things about the motifs that you hadn't realized? What were they, and how did they help your drawings?
2. Do you think your second or third drawings are better for each motif? Why?
3. Do you think your final drawing would look better if it were more stylized, or if it were more realistic? Why?

Worksheet 5-1. Finding motifs for a tile shape

For each tile shape below, think of a real-world motif that could be used for it, and draw in interior details. It may help to rotate the sheet to look at the shapes in different orientations and to consider different viewpoints (e.g., top view vs. side view).

Worksheet 5-2. Refining a tile shape using translation

For the tile shape below, from Worksheet 5-1, reshape the tile to improve your design from Worksheet 5-1. This tile has two distinct edges and fits together by translation. First reshape line a, then refine it, then reshape line b and refine it. At each stage, the two instances of line a must be identical, and similarly for line b. Each time you reshape a line, redraw the interior details, modifying your earlier details to fit the new shape.

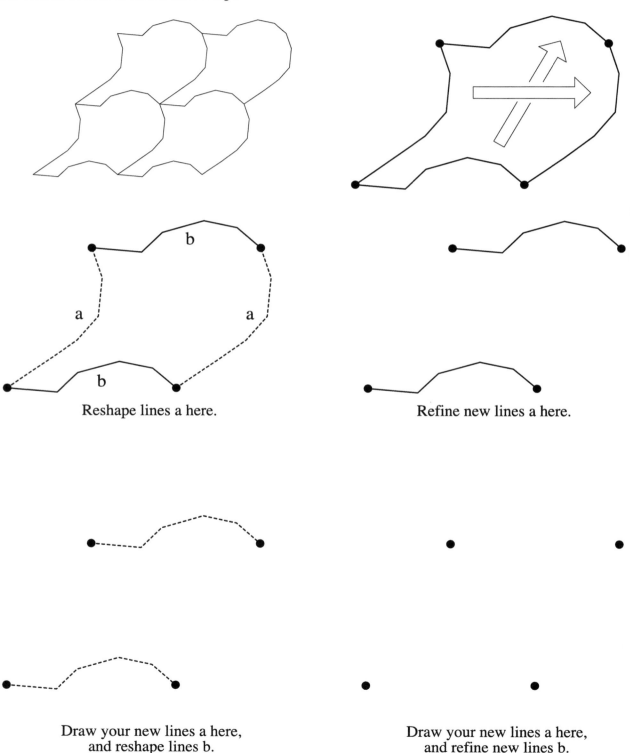

Reshape lines a here.

Refine new lines a here.

Draw your new lines a here,
and reshape lines b.

Draw your new lines a here,
and refine new lines b.

Worksheet 5-3. Refining a tile shape using glide reflection

For the tile shape below, from Worksheet 5-1, reshape the tile to improve your design from Worksheet 5-1. This tile has two distinct edges and fits together laterally by translation and vertically by glide reflection. First reshape line a, then refine it, then reshape line b and refine it. At each stage, the two instances of line b must be related by a reflection about a vertical line. This makes drawing the two instances of line b much trickier. Each time you reshape a line, redraw the interior details, modifying your earlier details to fit the new shape.

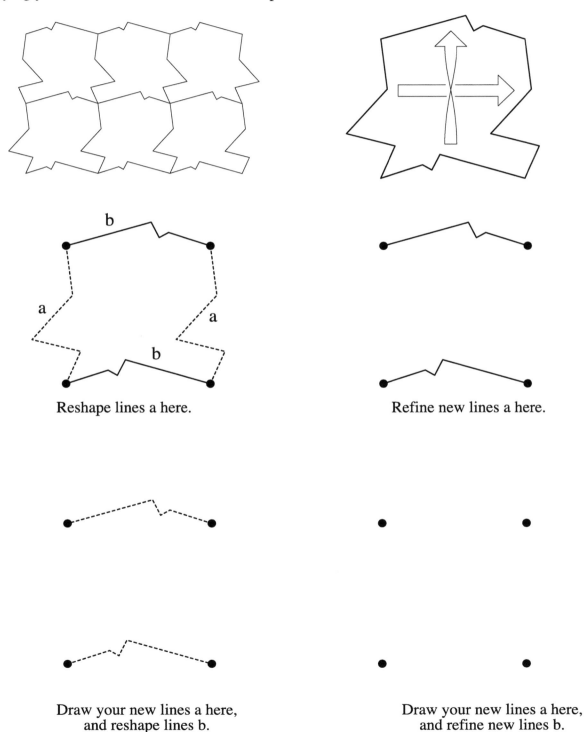

Reshape lines a here.

Refine new lines a here.

Draw your new lines a here,
and reshape lines b.

Draw your new lines a here,
and refine new lines b.

Worksheet 5-4. Locating and using source material for real-life motifs

For each tile shape below, first draw interior details in the leftmost outlines without using source material. Then search in books or on the Internet for images of the motif given. Try to find at least three images for each motif that show it from a similar viewpoint to that shown below. Using those images to guide you, draw in interior details in the middle outline. Compare your drawing to the images you found and decide how your drawing could be improved. Consider the degree to which the details are stylized vs. being realistic. Then draw interior details again in the rightmost outline.

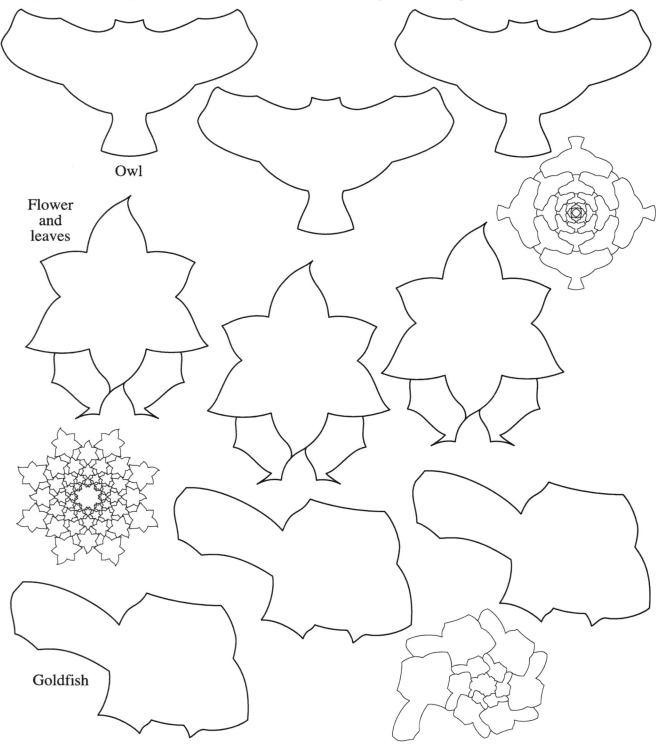

Owl

Flower and leaves

Goldfish

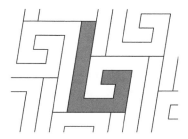

Special Techniques for Solving Design Problems

Producing a good tessellation generally takes hours of refinement. If you get stuck, do something else for a while and then come back to it. Coming back to a design after taking a break for hours or even days allows you a fresh and more objective look at it, and you will usually see a way to improve it. In writing this book, I looked back at tessellations I had designed years earlier and saw ways to improve many of them. The example below shows some steps in a seahorse tessellation that I first designed in the early 1992, wasn't satisfied with, and came back to a few times over the years till making the final version in 2008.

Sometimes you just can't get a tile to look right with the motif and the starting geometric tiling you've chosen. There are some special tricks that can help you out in such cases. Four of these techniques are described in this chapter, along with examples.

An early refinement

A later revision

Original design

Final design

Technique 1: Distorting the entire tessellation.

An entire tessellation can be stretched or skewed to change the shape of the tiles. This can be used to improve the appearance of Escheresque tiles. For example, if you create a tessellation of rabbits, and they look too short and squat, you can stretch them in the vertical direction.

Similarly, skewing a tessellation (pushing one side, while leaving the opposing side fixed) can be used to modify the appearance of the tiles, as shown with the chameleon tessellation below. One of the advantages to working on a computer is the ease with which distortions of this sort can be carried out.

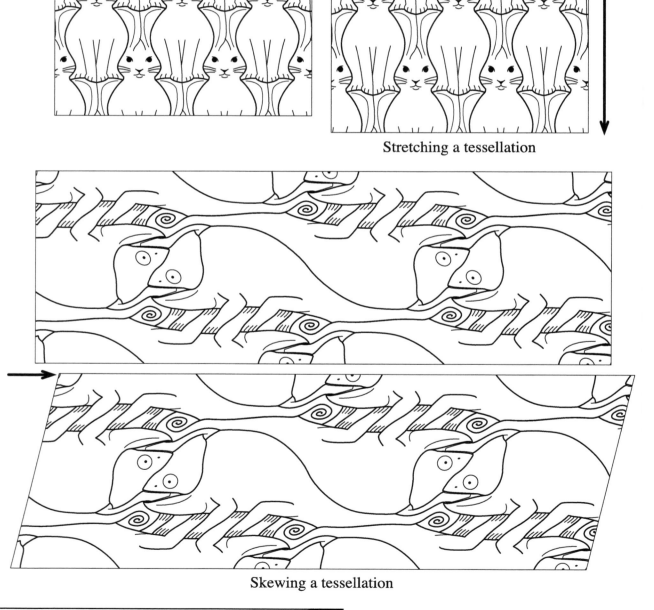

Stretching a tessellation

Skewing a tessellation

Technique 2: Breaking symmetries

For some motifs, a highly symmetric drawing may not allow tiles to fit together without gaps. Making a basically symmetric object not quite symmetric can solve this problem and make the tiles look more interesting as well. An example is the pteranodon tile and tessellation below. A pteranodon, like many living things, possesses bilateral symmetry. Drawn symmetrically, the beak and tail get in the way of one another. Tilting each to the side a bit allows them to fit together without leaving gaps or having to use an excessively short beak. Arriving at these pteranodon tiles from a simple starting tessellation of rhombi involves moving and splitting vertices, described in Technique 4.

Another examples is provided by the flower tessellation below. The flowers at bottom left have six-fold rotational symmetry, and each petal has bilateral symmetry. They nearly fit together, but small gaps remain between them. Modifying the petals in a way that removes their bilateral symmetry allows the flowers to tessellate. Note that the six-fold rotational symmetry is maintained.

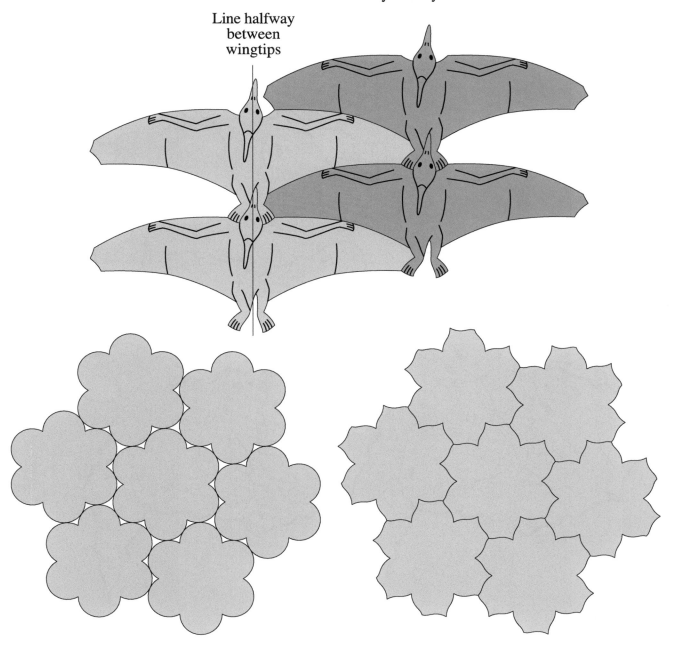

Line halfway
between
wingtips

Technique 3: Splitting a tile into two or more smaller tiles.

Sometimes you want to use a particular tile, but can't figure find a good motif for it. The tiling below has a unit cell of eight tiles, outlined with a heavy line, in which four different tiles each appear two times. The tile shapes are shown at upper left. At upper right, three of the four have had interior details added to form frogs, toads, and snakes. The last tile could be made into another snake, but the shape really wouldn't make a very good snake. A better solution is to divide it in two, as shown at lower left, after which interior details can be added to form two tadpoles, as shown at lower right. Escher used this technique in several of his tessellations. In the example here, the tile is divided into two smaller tiles of the same type. When Escher used this technique, he generally divided a tile into two different tiles.

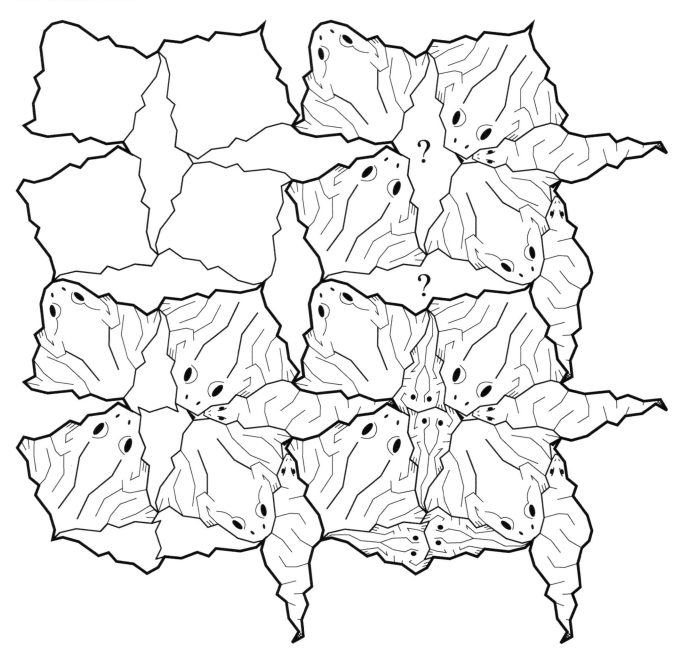

Technique 4: Splitting and moving vertices.

A very effective way of reshaping tiles in order to improve their shapes is to split and move vertices. This way, you are not constrained to rigidly conforming to your starting geometric template.

As an example, consider the pteranodon tessellation at top right. Let's say you aren't satisfied with the motif and wish you had more freedom in shaping the beak and back feet. You can achieve this by splitting and moving the vertex marked "a" so that it is replaced with the two vertices marked "b". Note that each tile has four vertices, all of the same type. This means that every vertex will split and move the same way.

The middle drawing shows how this affects the geometric tessellation underlying the design. Each rhombus is replaced by a hexagon, and each tile now has six vertices instead of four. You are now free to reshape the horizontal lines between the two new vertices any way you wish. In the bottom drawing, these have been reshaped to allow a longer beak and feet that extend out. The other edges were modified as well, creating a more realistic pteranodon.

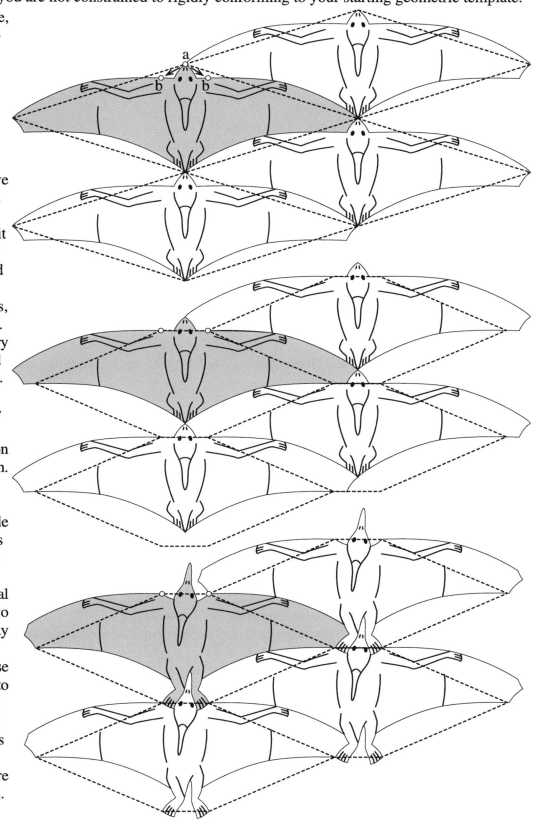

Activities

Activity 6-1. Splitting a tile into two smaller tiles

Materials: Copies of Worksheet 6-1.

Objective: Learn to improve a tessellation by splitting a tile into two smaller tiles.

Activity Sequence:
1. Pass out copies of the worksheet.
2. Go over the example at the top of the page.
3. Have students draw in interior details in the middle tiles, first working through an approach using the left pair of tiles, and then making a more polished drawing using the right pair of tiles.
4. Have students make the lower tiles into Escheresque tiles, first trying some different ways of dividing the left tile in two and adding interior details, then choosing an approach and making a more polished drawing using the right tile.

Discussion Questions:
1. Did you find it difficult to make the middle tiles into a frog and a fish? Why or why not?
2. How did you divide up the lower tile? Do you think your design was effective? Why or why not?
3. Did anyone divide the tile up differently? If so, compare the two approaches.

Activity 6-2. Reshaping a tile by splitting and moving vertices

Materials: Copies of Worksheet 6-2.

Objective: Learn to improve the shape of an Escheresque tile by splitting and moving vertices of the tessellation.

Vocabulary: Vertex (plural form vertices)

Activity Sequence:
1. Write the vocabulary term on the board and review its meaning.
2. Pass out copies of the worksheet.
3. Go over the top portion of the worksheet, making sure the students understand steps 1 and 2.
4. Have students redraw the tile as directed in step 3, with the side vertices split and moved. Be sure all of the students modify the tile correctly, so it tessellates.
5. Have the students reshape the edges and add interior details, as directed in step 4.

Discussion Questions:
1. Did you find it difficult to complete the reshaping of the tile in step 3? Why or why not?
2. How did you modify the edges in step 4? Do you think your design is effective? Why or why not?
3. Did anyone modify the edges differently? Compare and contrast the different approaches.

Worksheet 6-1. Splitting a tile into two smaller tiles

M.C. Escher often split a tile in two in order to form more attractive motifs. He did this several times with the rhombus below, where the opposing sides of the full rhombus are simply related by translation. The top example shows how he formed two bird tiles in this manner. The middle example shows the outlines of two tiles he formed by splitting a tile of this sort. He used interior details to make these into a frog and a fish. See if you can do the same. The lower example shows an undivided large tile. Escher divided this into two tiles, one of which he made into a fish and the other a bird. Again, see if you can do the same. For the middle and lower examples, there are two copies of each, so you can work out your approach and then make final drawings.

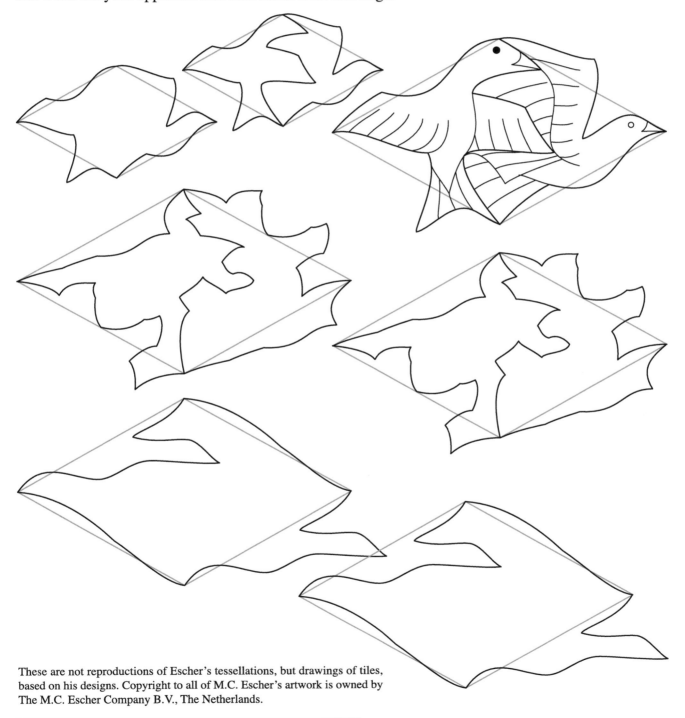

These are not reproductions of Escher's tessellations, but drawings of tiles, based on his designs. Copyright to all of M.C. Escher's artwork is owned by The M.C. Escher Company B.V., The Netherlands.

Worksheet 6-2. Reshaping a tile by splitting and moving vertices

Suppose you made the butterfly tessellation at right, but weren't satisfied with it. Perhaps you think it would be improved if there were a way to shorten the body and make the wings bigger. The steps below walk you through using the technique of splitting and moving vertices to achieve this goal.

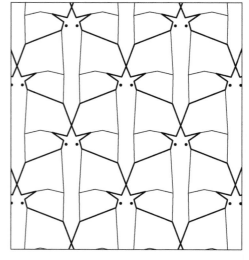

1. The butterfly tile is based on a tessellation of rhombi. Each tile has four vertices, all of the same type. Suppose you decide to try moving the top vertex down and the bottom vertex up, as shown.

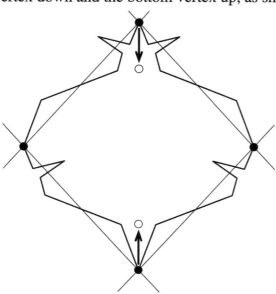

2. As a starting point, suppose you move all of the points close to the top vertex down by the same amount, and the points close to the bottom vertex up by the same amount. This reshapes the tile as shown, making the body shorter, but the wings are too small now.

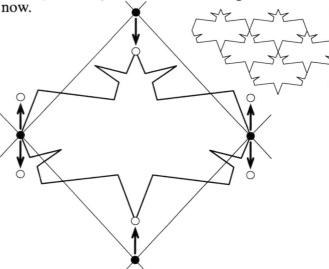

3. Redraw the tile with the side vertices split and moved, and the nearby points moved as well, so that the new tile tessellates. The lightly dashed lines will all be changed. Note that the underlying geometric template is now a tessellation of hexagons.

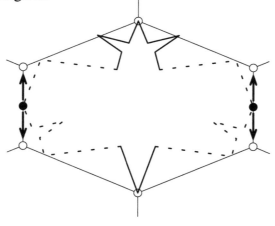

4. Now reshape the edges to improve the appearance of the motif, maintaining a shape that will tessellate. Draw in interior details as well.

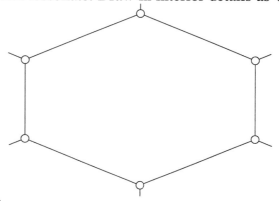

Tessellations Based on Square Tiles

A grid of squares is the simplest geometric basis for a tessellation and therefore a good starting point in learning to design tessellations. At the same time, a square grid offers a wide range of possibilities, including tessellations with translational, rotational, and glide reflection symmetries.

In this chapter, templates are presented that provide examples of each type of symmetry. Square grids are provided that can be used to guide the design of tessellations using hand drawing and cutting techniques. Every template and example in this chapter uses a square grid of this scale. A detailed step-by-step example shows how to use the templates and grids to create your own tessellation designs. The same general procedure can be used with the templates in later chapters.

On the template pages in this and subsequent chapters, distinct line segments are labeled a, b, etc., and the flag next to the letter shows the orientation of that particular line segment. The arrow from one edge of the tile to another indicates how the line segment transforms, by translation, rotation, or reflection. The tessellation formed is shown on the lower half of the template page, along with a description of how to draw it. Hands denote the different tiles and orientations within the tessellation. A hand with a single upheld finger indicates the first prototile of the tessellation, while two fingers indicates the second prototile. The orientation of the hands indicates the orientation of the tiles, while Roman numerals next to the hands enumerate distinct orientations of the tile.

The templates can be used either to create tessellations by hand or using a drawing program on a computer. The detailed example in this chapter shows how to create a tessellation by hand, but it is straightforward to mimic these steps using a computer drawing program.

M.C. Escher utilized square grids in many of his tessellations. In his famous 1939-1940 woodcut *Metamorphose II*, lizards emerge from a checkerboard pattern of black and white squares. Other motifs he formed using square grids include ants, angels and devils (two of each per square), and fish.

While a square grid is the easiest geometric basis to work with, from a graphics design standpoint square grids can lead to designs that are blocky or static, lacking motion and life. This is particularly true in a tessellation that only possesses translational symmetry. This doesn't have to be the case, but it's something to be aware of and to be consciously avoided.

A closely-related geometric basis is a grid of rectangles. These are not treated as a separate topic in this book, but many of the square templates presented in this chapter and the next can be made into rectangular templates simply by stretching the design in one direction, as described in Chapter 5.

Creating a Tessellation by Hand

This detailed example uses the square grids and Template 7-3 found later in this chapter. It illustrates a general method for designing tessellations by hand using the various templates in this book.

Step 1. Copy the Square Tile Grids sheet onto a heavy paper, such as card stock. Copy the Square Tessellation Grid sheet onto a lighter paper that works well for drawing and coloring.

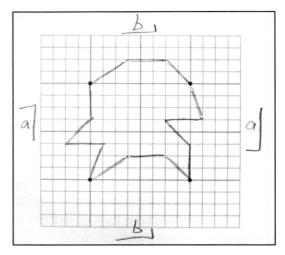

Step 2. For the template chosen, mark the appropriate letters and flags showing the relationship between the various sides of the shape (a square in this case). Do this for each of the tile grids. Note that for some templates, you will have two different tiles. In this case, you may to draw each one on a separate tile grid, depending on the grid used.

Step 3. Using these markings as a guide, draw curves (these can consist of straight-line segments) that follow the rules indicated by the letters and flags. The large arrows on the template sheets show how a line segment moves from one edge to another. It is probably easiest to start by connecting crossing points on the grid with straight-line segments, as shown in the top figure at right.

Step 4. If your shape suggests a motif that you wish to develop further, refine the shape of your curves on the same or a fresh tile grid. You may wish to rough in interior details at this point, as shown in the middle figure at right. If you don't like your shape (your tile), you may wish to try all new starting curves.

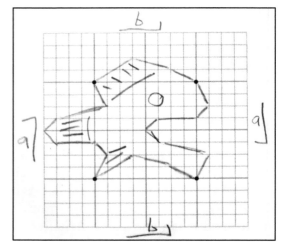

Step 5. Once you are satisfied with the tentative outline, refine it further and draw in interior details, as shown in the bottom figure at right. This is what each tile in your tessellation will look like. Keep the orientation of the tiles in the final tessellation in mind. For example, for the template chosen here, half the fishes would be upside down. This can be avoided by drawing different interior details for those tiles, as shown in the bottom figure at left, where the upside-down tile has been split into two smaller tiles.

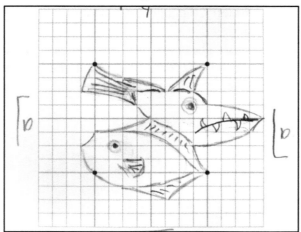

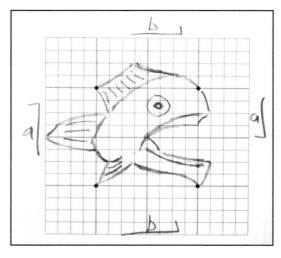

Step 6. Once you are satisfied with your tile, carefully cut curves as instructed on the template sheet. In the example here, cut one of the two "a" curves, and one of the two "b" curves. Cut off the bulk of the sheet, so you have a piece similar to that shown at top, right, that can used as a tracing template.

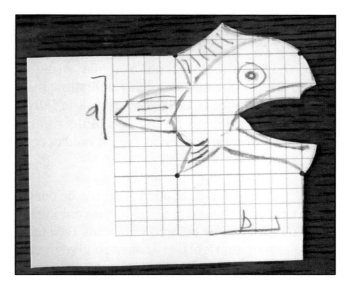

Step 7. Use this template to draw a tile on the appropriate tessellation grid sheet. Carefully align the shape to the grid using the dots. Hold it firmly in place and tightly trace the cut curves, as shown at middle right. It's important to use a sharp pencil and trace right at the edge of the template. Then reposition the template to trace the other curves. The template page shows how the tiles fit together, and how each tile is oriented. Use it as a guide to ensure the curves are traced in the correct orientations. Template 7-3 shows that both the "a" and "b" curves are oriented the same within a column, but that they are mirrored from one column to the adjacent column. This means the template needs to flipped over to draw these curves, as shown at bottom, right.

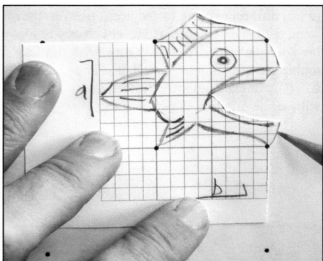

Step 8. Repeat this process of aligning the template with dots and tracing the template until the entire tessellation grid sheet (or as much as you want) is covered with your tessellated shapes.

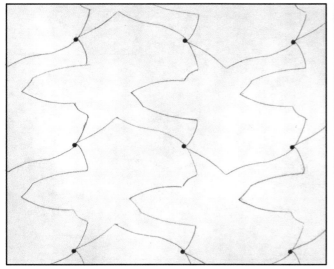

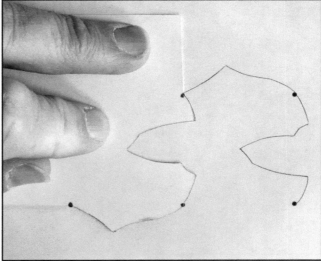

Step 9. Lightly draw in the key interior lines using a pencil, as shown at top, right.

Step 10. Draw the final lines. You may wish to use an ink pen for this step. This will allow the pencil marks to be erased once the ink is fully dry, as shown in the figure at middle right. Otherwise, smearing of pencil marks could occur during coloring.

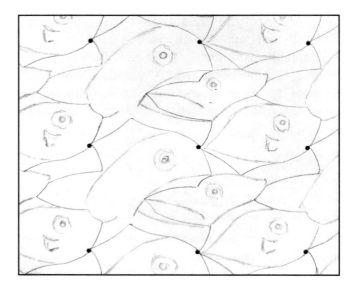

Step 11. Color your tessellation. This can be done using crayons, colored pencils, felt-tip markers, etc. The tiles can be colored uniformly (see the figure at bottom, right), or shaded to give them more of a three-dimensional appearance (see the figure at bottom, left). It is usually a good idea to use different colors for adjacent tiles, so they stand out better. Choose whatever colors you like for your particular tiles. You may wish to make multiple copies of your tessellation after Step 10, so you can experiment with different colorings without having to redraw the tiles.

Square Tile Grids

Use these grids to design tiles using the templates found in Chapter 7. First choose a template, then copy the letters and flags for each line segment on a grid. Then draw curves (these can consist of straight-line segments) connecting the dots in a manner that follows the rules described by the letters and flags. Make sure the curves won't cross anywhere in the full tessellation. If you find a tile you like, refine the shape of the curves and add interior details to create a motif for your tessellation. Then cut out your tile as directed on the template page, and follow the directions there to form a tessellation on a copy of the Square Tessellation Grid (p. 76).

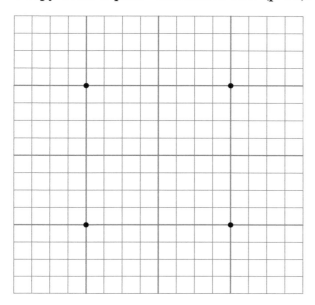
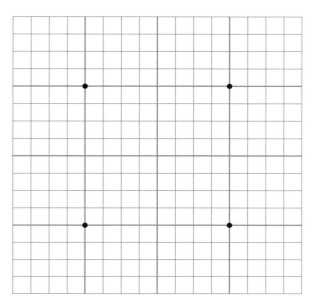

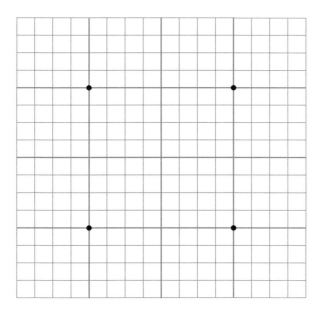
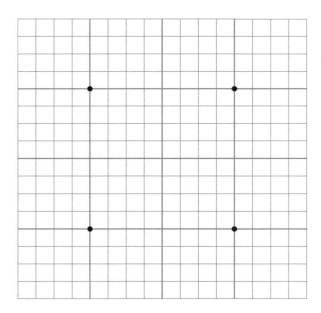

Symmetry group p1, Heesch type TTTT, Escher's notebook nos. 105, 106, 127, and 128

Tessellation with translational symmetry only

This is the simplest way to form a tessellation using a square grid. There are two independent line segments, each of which simply translates from one side of the square to the other.

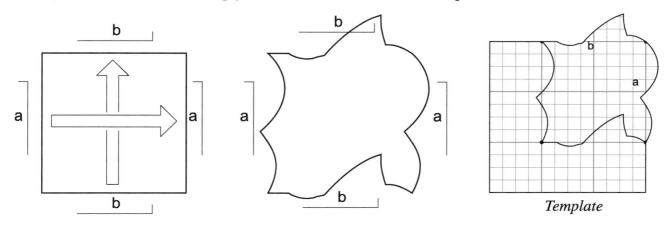

Template

To draw this tessellation using the grids:
Cut along the top and right edges of your tile. Form Line 1 as indicated below by tracing the cut edges.
Repeatedly draw this same line in the same orientation to form a larger tessellation.

Tessellation with 2- and 4-fold rotational symmetry

This is another simple template, but one that forms a more interesting tessellation, with both 2-fold and 4-fold rotational symmetry. The tile appears in four different orientations in the tessellation.

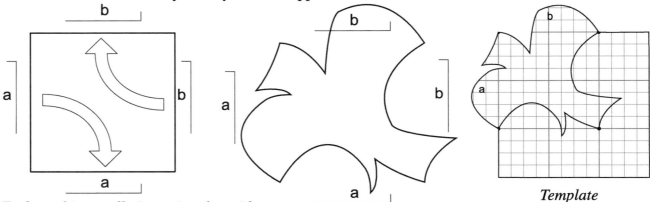

Template

To draw this tessellation using the grids:
Cut along the top and left edges of your tile. Form Line 1 as indicated below by tracing the cut edges. Then rotate your template 90° clockwise and form Line 2. Rotate clockwise 90° again to form Line 3, and one last time to form Line 4. Repeat this group of four lines to form a larger tessellation.

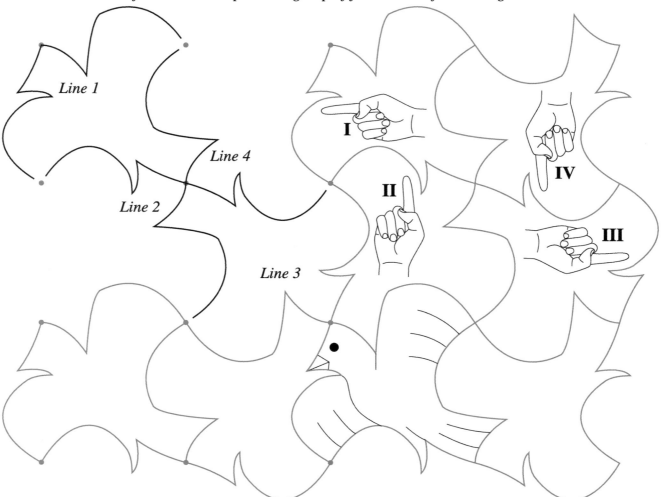

"Four-fold Seahorses"

This tessellation is based on Template 7-2. Using the squares to guide you, try drawing additional tiles on the top row. Then add details to these and to the blank tiles in the second row. You can also color the tessellation or mark the points of rotational symmetry. How many colors are required if no two adjacent tiles are to have the same color?

"Seahorses and Eels"

This tessellation is also based on Template 7-2. In this design, each tile has been divided into two smaller tiles. Using the squares to guide you, try drawing additional tiles on the top row. Then add details to these and the blank tiles in the upper left quadrant below. You can also color the tessellation or mark the points of rotational symmetry.

Tessellation with glide reflection symmetry

One of two independent line segments simply translates from one side of the square to the opposite edge, while the other line segment is reflected from one side of the square to the other. This results in a tessellation possessing glide reflection symmetry, in which the tile appears in two distinct orientations.

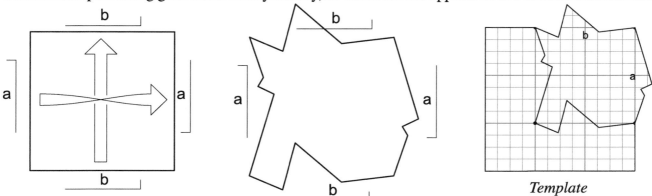

To draw this tessellation using the grids:
Cut along the top and right edges of your tile. Form Column 1 of lines as indicated below by tracing the cut edges. Then flip your template over top to bottom and form an adjacent Column 2 of lines. Repeat this pattern to make a wider tessellation.

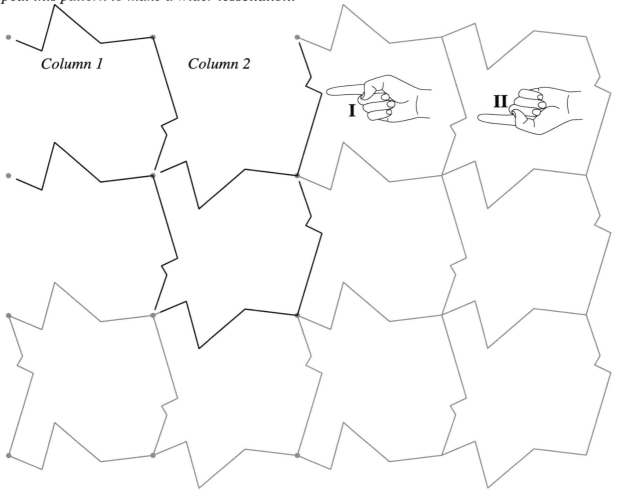

Tessellation with glide reflection symmetry

This tessellation only has one independent line segment, but multiple lines of glide reflection symmetry. The motif, which possesses bilateral symmetry, appears in four different orientations.

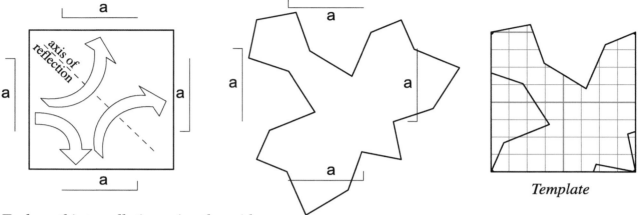

Template

To draw this tessellation using the grids:
Cut along the top edge of your tile. Form Line 1 as indicated below by tracing the cut edge. Then rotate your template 90° counter-clockwise to form Line 2. Next flip it over top to bottom to trace Line 3. Finally rotate it 90° clockwise to form Line 4. Form lines 5-8 as shown and then repeat this group of lines to form a larger tessellation.

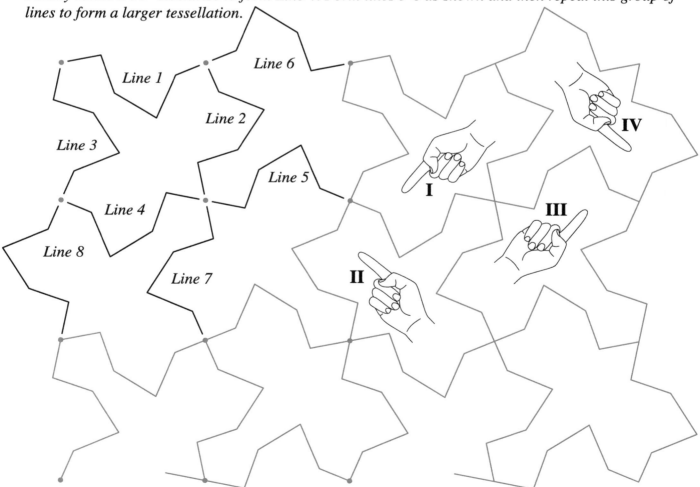

Tessellation with rotational and glide reflection symmetry

Each of two distinct line segments is reflected from one side of the square to the other, resulting in a tessellation possessing both 2-fold rotational symmetry and two distinct lines of glide reflection symmetry. The tile appears in four orientations.

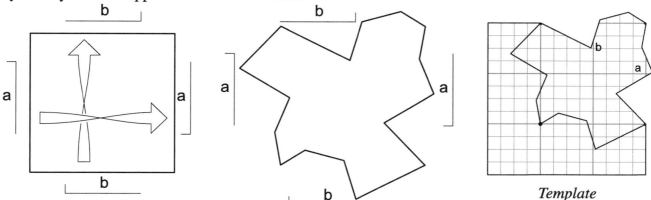

Template

To draw this tessellation using the grids:
Cut along the top and right edges of your tile. Form Line 1 as indicated below by tracing the cut edges. Then flip your template over right to left and form Line 2. Next flip it over top to bottom and form Line 3. Then flip it over right to left and form Line 4. Repeat this group of four lines to form a larger tessellation.

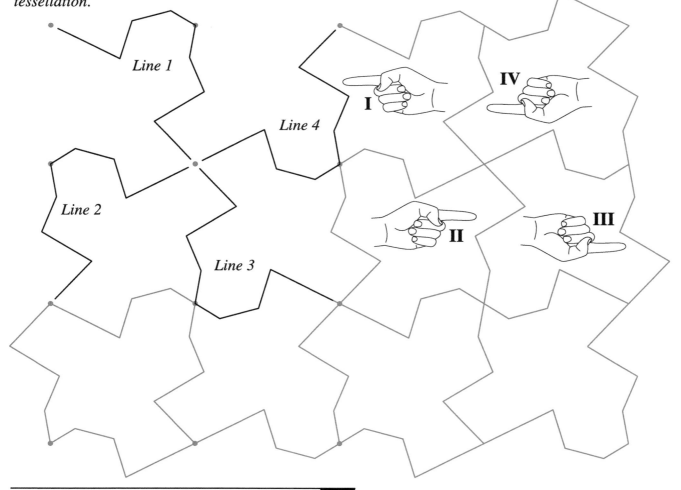

Tessellation with 2-fold rotational and glide reflection symmetry

This template contains a bilaterally symmetric tile that occurs in two different orientations. There are two independent line segments, each of which occurs four times in a tile.

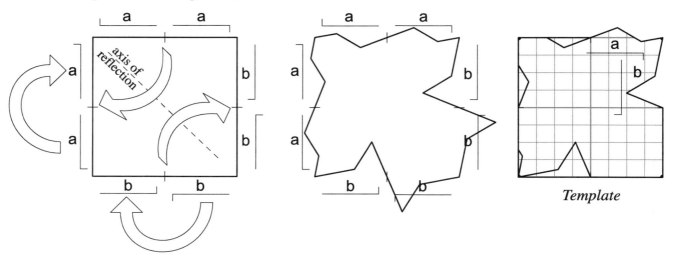

Template

To draw this tessellation using the grids:
Cut along the right half of the top edge and the top half of the right edge of your tile. Form Line 1 as indicated below by tracing along the cut edges. Then rotate your template 180° and form Line 2. Next, flip it over about a diagonal line running from the top left to bottom right corners of the tile and form Line 3. Finally, rotate it 180° and form Line 4. Repeat this group of four lines to form the larger tessellation.

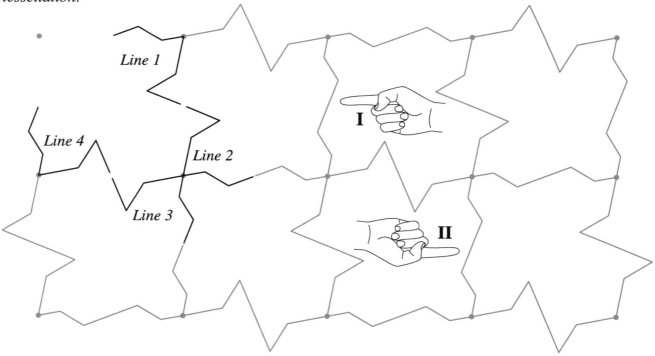

Tessellation with two motifs and glide reflection symmetry

This template has two motifs, each of which occurs in two orientations, and glide reflection symmetry. This is the same template used for the Cats and Mice design earlier in the book, except it is stretched vertically for that design.

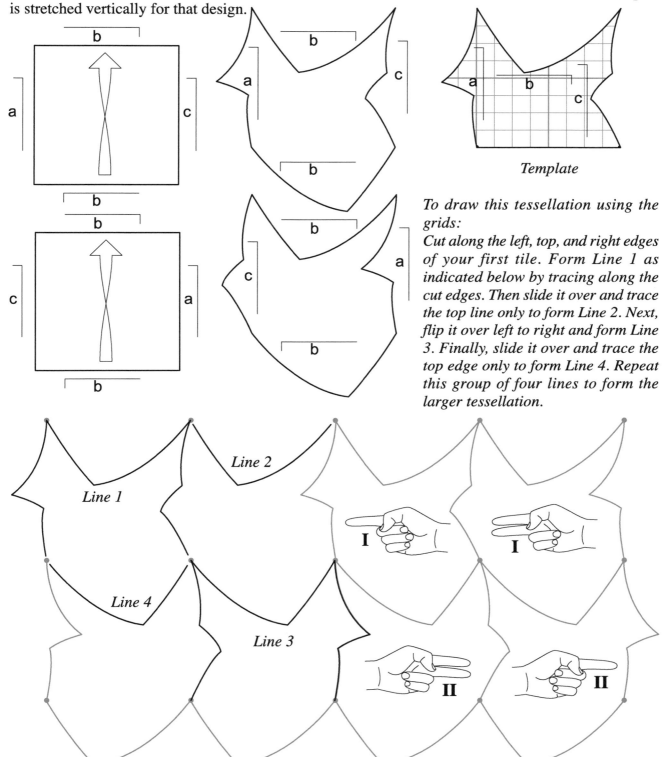

Template

To draw this tessellation using the grids:
Cut along the left, top, and right edges of your first tile. Form Line 1 as indicated below by tracing along the cut edges. Then slide it over and trace the top line only to form Line 2. Next, flip it over left to right and form Line 3. Finally, slide it over and trace the top edge only to form Line 4. Repeat this group of four lines to form the larger tessellation.

Tessellation with two different tiles and reflection symmetry

This template contains two different tiles, each of which possess reflection symmetry about a center line. This sort of symmetry lends itself well to living creatures seen from top or front views.

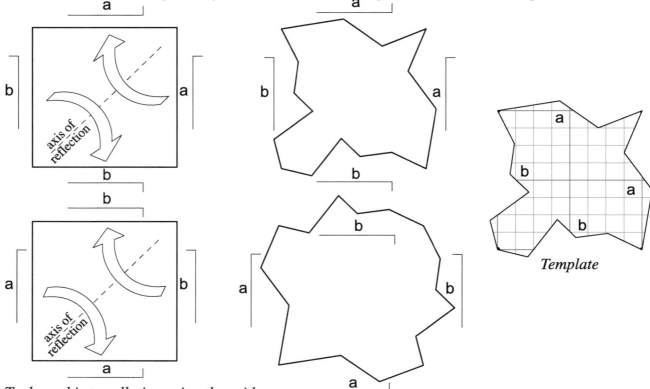

Template

To draw this tessellation using the grids:
Completely cut out your top tile. Form Line 1 as indicated below by tracing all the way around your template. Translate your template and trace completely around it to form Line 2. Repeat to form a larger tessellation.

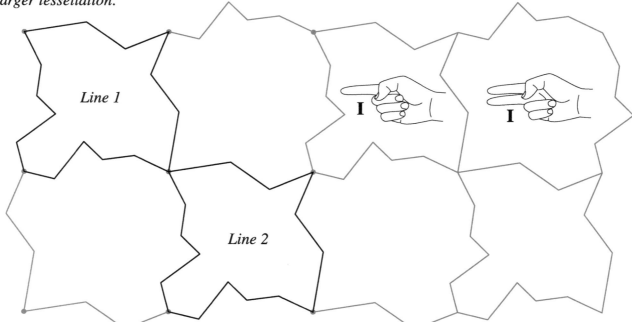

Tessellation with two different tiles and reflection symmetry

This template contains two different tiles. The tessellation contains multiple lines of reflection and glide reflection symmetry, as well as points of 2- and 4-fold rotational symmetry. A single line segment appears 8 times in each tile.

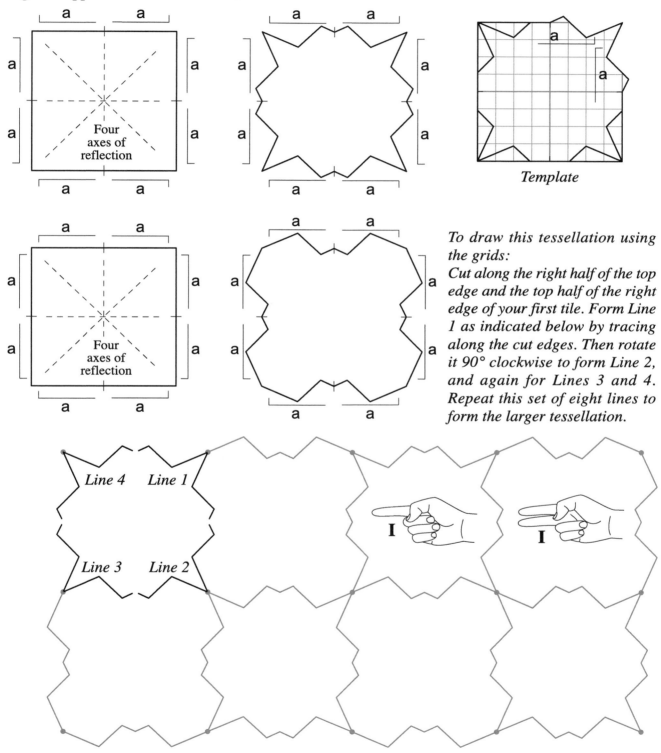

Four axes of reflection

Template

Four axes of reflection

To draw this tessellation using the grids:
Cut along the right half of the top edge and the top half of the right edge of your first tile. Form Line 1 as indicated below by tracing along the cut edges. Then rotate it 90° clockwise to form Line 2, and again for Lines 3 and 4. Repeat this set of eight lines to form the larger tessellation.

Line 4   Line 1

Line 3   Line 2

"Flowers I"

This flower design is based on Template 7-9. Try finishing the top two rows of the tessellation. Where are the lines of glide reflection symmetry (ignoring small differences in interior details) and points of rotational symmetry?

Some of M.C. Escher's most famous tessellations are based on a square grid. Many of these can be produced using the templates in this chapter. Some of the tiles he created in this category are shown below. Can you tell which template could be used to produce each of these tiles?

These are not reproductions of Escher's tessellations, but drawings of tiles, based on his designs, that can be creating using the grids provided. Copyright to all of M.C. Escher's artwork is owned by The M.C. Escher Company B.V., The Netherlands.

Activities

The steps below are described in more detail in the pages on creating a tessellation by hand (pp. 72-74). Unless otherwise noted, a pencil should be used. In a classroom setting, the teacher may wish to demonstrate the steps before having the students perform them.

Activity 7-1. Creating a tessellation with translational symmetry

Materials: Copies of template sheet 7-1 on copier paper, copies of the Square Tile Grids sheet on card stock, copies of the Square Tessellation Grid sheet on a paper that can be drawn and colored on, scissors or craft knife, pencil, pen, eraser, crayons or colored pencils (or other means of coloring a tessellation).

Objective: Learn to create, by hand, a tessellation that possesses translational symmetry.

Vocabulary: Translational symmetry, template, vector, tile, prototile, motif.

Activity Sequence:
1. Write the vocabulary words on the board and discuss the meaning of each.
2. Pass out the copies and other materials.
3. On the bottom portion of the template sheet, have the students draw two different vectors indicating translation distances and directions that would cause the tessellation to perfectly overlap itself.
4. Have the students mark the letters and flags for each of the four Square Tile Grids in a similar fashion to how they're marked on the template sheet.
5. Using the letters and flags as a guide, have them draw curves connecting the grid dots on at least one of the grids. The two "a" lines should be identical, as should the two "b" lines.
6. Have the students identify a motif in (one of) their shape(s). Then have them refine the shape and rough in interior details.
7. Have them further refine the shape and interior details to produce a prototile.
8. Have them cut out one curve of each type (one for each letter) and cut off the bulk of the sheet to create a template, as shown on the template sheet.
9. Have them use their templates to draw the outlines of the tiles on the Square Tessellation Grid sheet, as directed on the Template 7-1 sheet, continuing until the sheet is filled up.
10. Have them lightly sketch in key interior details for each tile.
11. Have the students use an ink pen to go over the tile outlines and interior details for the entire tessellation. After the ink is fully dry, unwanted pencil marks can be erased.
12. Have them color their tessellations. Before starting, you may wish to discuss coloring options.

Discussion Questions:
1. What motif did you use for your tile? Do you think it was effective? How would you change it if you could do it over again?
2. What step did you find the most challenging? Why?

Activity 7-2. Creating a tessellation with rotational symmetry

Materials: Copies of template sheet 7-2 on copier paper, copies of the Square Tile Grids sheet on card stock, copies of the Square Tessellation Grid sheet on a paper that can be drawn and colored on, scissors or craft knife, pencil, pen, eraser, crayons or colored pencils (or other means of coloring a tessellation).

Objective: Learn to create, by hand, a tessellation that possesses rotational symmetry.

Vocabulary: Rotational symmetry.

Activity Sequence:
1. Write the vocabulary term on the board and discuss its meaning.
2. Pass out the copies and other materials.
3. On the bottom portion of the template sheet, have the students mark each distinct point of rotational symmetry, using a polygon to indicate the amount of rotation. For 2-fold rotation, use a rectangle. For 4-fold rotation, use a square.
4. Have the students mark the letters and flags for each of the four Square Tile Grids in a similar fashion to how they're marked on the template sheet.
5. Using the letters and flags as a guide, have them draw curves connecting the grid dots on at least one of the grids. The two "a" lines should be identical, as should the two "b" lines.
6. Have the students identify a motif in (one of) their shape(s). Then have them refine the shape and rough in interior details.
7. Have them further refine the shape and interior details to produce a prototile.
8. Have them cut out one curve of each type (one for each letter) and cut off the bulk of the sheet to create a template, as shown on the template sheet.
9. Have them use their templates to draw the outlines of the tiles on the Square Tessellation Grid sheet, as directed on the Template 7-2 sheet, continuing until the sheet is filled up.
10. Have them lightly sketch in key interior details for each tile.
11. Have the students use an ink pen to go over the tile outlines and interior details for the entire tessellation. After the ink is fully dry, unwanted pencil marks can be erased.
12. Have them color their tessellations. Before starting, you may wish to discuss coloring options.

Discussion Questions:
1. What motif did you use for your tile? Do you think it was effective? How would you change it if you could do it over again?
2. What step did you find the most challenging? Why?
3. Did you find designing this tessellation to be more or less difficult than designing the tessellation in Activity 7-1? Why?

Activity 7-3. Creating a tessellation with glide reflection symmetry

Materials: Copies of template sheet 7-3 on copier paper, copies of the Square Tile Grids sheet on card stock, copies of the Square Tessellation Grid sheet on a paper that can be drawn and colored on, scissors or craft knife, pencil, pen, eraser, crayons or colored pencils (or other means of coloring a tessellation).

Objective: Learn to create, by hand, a tessellation that possesses glide reflection symmetry.

Vocabulary: Glide-reflection symmetry.

Activity Sequence:
1. Write the vocabulary term on the board and discuss its meaning.
2. Pass out the copies and other materials.
3. On the bottom portion of the template sheet, have the students mark the lines of glide reflection symmetry, along with glide vectors that cause the tessellation to perfectly overlie itself.
4. Have the students mark the letters and flags for each of the four Square Tile Grids in a similar fashion to how they're marked on the template sheet.
5. Using the letters and flags as a guide, have them draw curves connecting the grid dots on at least one of the grids. The two "b" lines should be identical, while the two "a" lines should be mirror images of each other.
6. Have the students identify a motif in (one of) their shape(s). Then have them refine the shape and rough in interior details.
7. Have them further refine the shape and interior details to produce a prototile.
8. Have them cut out one curve of each type (one for each letter) and cut off the bulk of the sheet to create a template, as shown on the template sheet.
9. Have them use their templates to draw the outlines of the tiles on the Square Tessellation Grid sheet, as directed on the Template 7-3 sheet, continuing until the sheet is filled up.
10. Have them lightly sketch in key interior details for each tile.
11. Have the students use an ink pen to go over the tile outlines and interior details for the entire tessellation. After the ink is fully dry, unwanted pencil marks can be erased.
12. Have them color their tessellations. Before starting, you may wish to discuss coloring options.

Discussion Questions:
1. What motif did you use for your tile? Do you think it was effective? How would you change it if you could do it over again?
2. What step did you find the most challenging? Why?
3. Did you find designing this tessellation to be more or less difficult than designing the tessellations in Activities 7-1 and 7-2? Why?
4. Which of the three templates, 7-1, 7-2, or 7-3, is your favorite? Why?

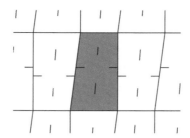

Other Tiles Based on a Square Grid

In this chapter some tessellations based on right triangle and kite-shaped tiles are described. These can be drawn on the same Square Tessellation Grid in Chapter 7. Additional tile grids tailored to these shapes follow on the next page.

A right triangle is one that contains a "right" (90°) angle. The right triangles that are used as templates in this chapter also contain two 45° angles. Since two of the angles are the same, they can be described as right isosceles triangles. These can be obtained by simply dividing a square in two along a diagonal.

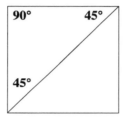

As described in Chapter 3, a kite is a quadrilateral with two adjacent sides of one length and two other adjacent sides of a second length, and all interior angles less than 180°. A few examples of different kites are shown below.

A kite template was used by Escher to form three of his most famous tessellations – geese, winged lions (used in the print *Magic Mirror*) and riders on horses (used in the print *Horsemen*). The shape of the kites he used are somewhat different in each design.

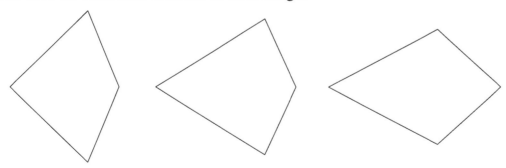

Right Triangle and Kite Tile Grids

Use these grids to design tiles using the templates found in Chapter 8. First choose a template, then copy the letters and flags for each line segment on one of the grids. Then draw curves (these can consist of straight-line segments) connecting the dots in a manner that follows the rules described by the letters and flags. Make sure the curves don't cross anywhere. If you find a tile you like, refine the shape of the curves and add interior details to create a motif for your tessellation. Then cut out your tile as directed on the template page, and follow the directions there to form a tessellation.

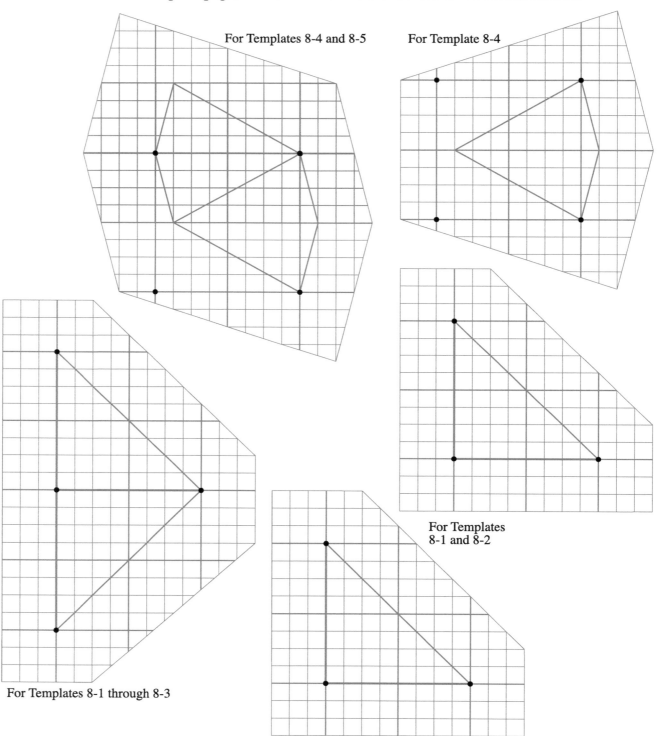

For Templates 8-4 and 8-5   For Template 8-4

For Templates 8-1 and 8-2

For Templates 8-1 through 8-3

Right-triangle tessellation with 2-fold rotational symmetry

This template divides the square grid in half along a diagonal, forming two right triangles. This tessellation has multiple distinct points of 2-fold rotational symmetry.

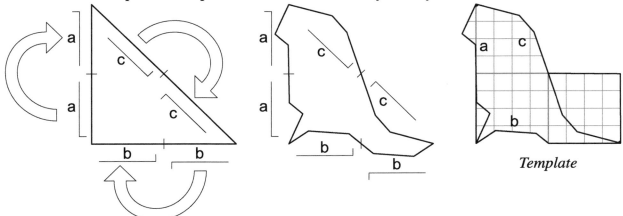

Template

To draw this tessellation using the grids:

To form your template, cut along three of the six curves making up your tile and cut the other three as straight lines, as shown above right. Form the first set of three lines by tracing the three curves with the template fixed in place. Then rotate the template 180° and form the second set of three lines, as shown below. Repeat this group of six lines to form a larger tessellation.

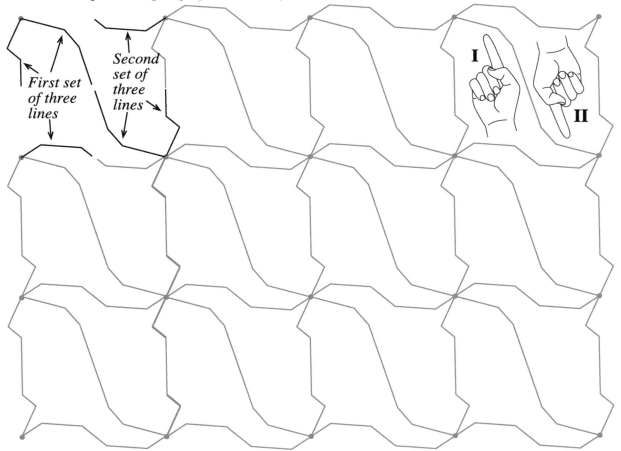

Right-triangle tessellation with 2- and 4-fold rotational symmetry

This template also divides the square grid in half along a diagonal, forming two right triangles. The tiles appears in four different orientations in the tessellation. There two distinct points of 4-fold rotational symmetry, with four motifs meeting at one of them and eight at the other.

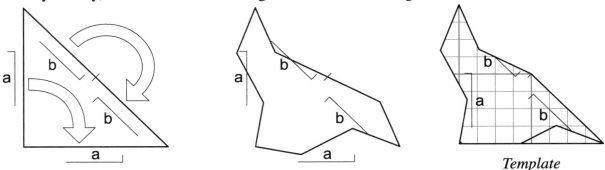

Template

To draw this tessellation using the grids:
Cut along the left edge and the top half of the diagonal of your tile, as shown above right. Form Line 1 as indicated below by tracing along the cut edges. Then rotate your template 180° to form Line 2. Next rotate 90° counter-clockwise to form Line 3. Finally, rotate 180° to form Line 4. Repeat this set of four lines to form a larger tessellation.

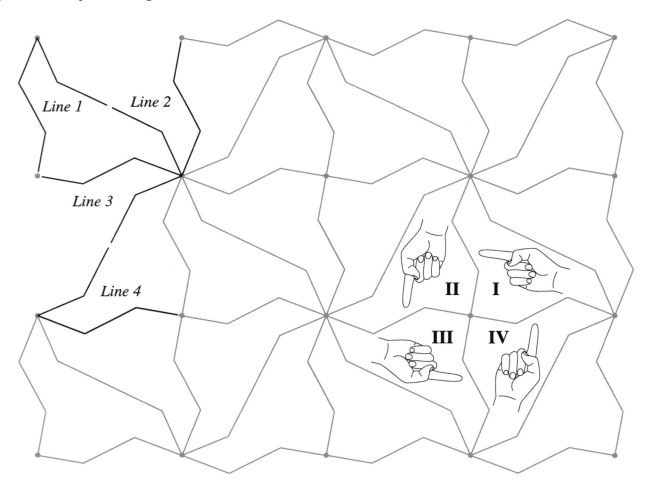

Right-triangle tessellation with 2- and 4-fold rotational and reflection symmetry

This template also divides the square grid in half along a diagonal, forming two right triangles. It has two different tiles, each of which appears in four different orientations. This template can be used to produce one of Escher's most famous tessellations, with angels and devils as the motifs.

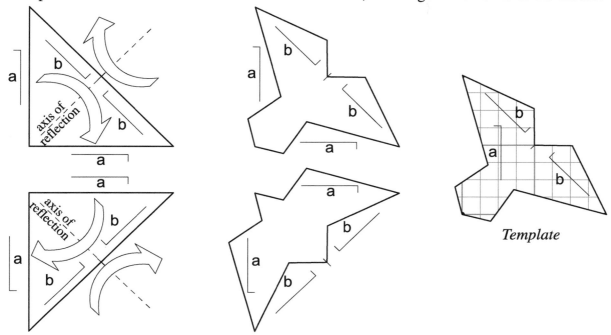

Template

To draw this tessellation using the grids:
Completely cut out your top tile, as shown above right. Form Line 1 as indicated below by tracing all the way around it. Then rotate it 90° counter-clockwise to form Line 2. Rotate another 90° to form Line 3, and another 90° to form Line 4. Repeat this set of four lines to form a larger tessellation.

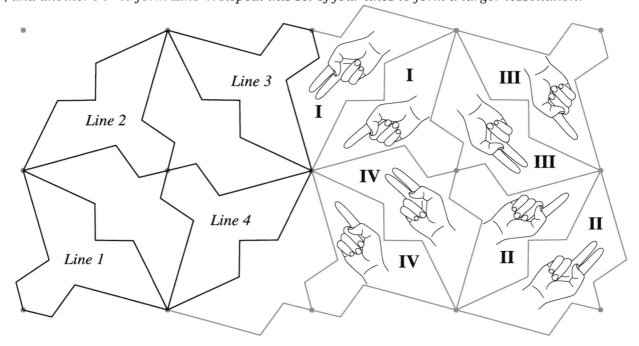

Kite tessellation with glide reflection symmetry

The particular kite shown here can be fit to a square grid. The lengths of the lines a and b can be varied by moving the points P and P' to the right or left, with the constraint that the distance from P to P' remain equal to the width of the square. Note that the two orientations of tiles in the tessellation line up with the grid dots differently.

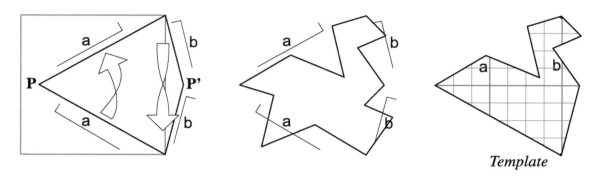

Template

To draw this tessellation using the grids:
Cut along the upper edges of your tile, as shown above right. Form Line 1 as indicated below by tracing along the cut edges. Then flip your template over left to right to form Line 2. Repeat this set of two lines to form a larger tessellation.

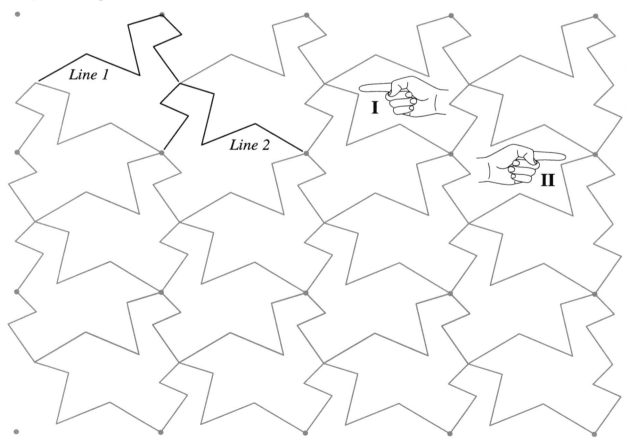

Kite tessellation with two motifs and glide reflection symmetry

This template has two different tiles, each of which appears in two orientations, mirrored with respect to each other.

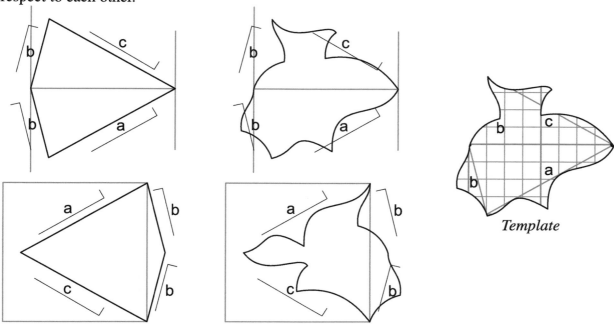

Template

To draw this tessellation using the grids:
Completely cut out your top tile, as shown above right. Form Line 1 as indicated below by tracing along the cut edges c and a. Then slide your template over and trace along the two b edges to form Line 2. Next flip your template over left to right and trace all around it to form Line 3. Repeat this set of three lines to form a larger tessellation.

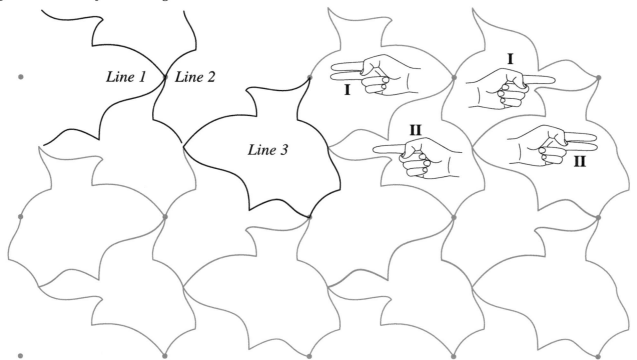

Activities

Activity 8-1. Creating a tessellation based on right-triangle tiles

Materials: Copies of template sheet 8-2 on copier paper, Right Triangle and Kite Tile Grids sheet on card stock, Square Tessellation Grid sheet on a paper that can be drawn and colored on, scissors or craft knife, pencil, pen, eraser, crayons or colored pencils (or other means of coloring a tessellation).

Objective: Learn to create a tessellation by hand based on right-triangle tiles.

Vocabulary: Right triangle, isosceles right triangle.

Activity Sequence:
1. Write the vocabulary terms on the board and discuss their meanings.
2. Pass out the copies and other materials.
3. On the bottom portion of the template sheet, have the students mark each distinct point of rotational symmetry, using a polygon to indicate the amount of rotation. For 2-fold rotation, use a rectangle. For 4-fold rotation, use a square.
4. Have the students mark the letters and flags for each of the three right triangle tile grids (the top half only of the double right-triangle grid) in a similar fashion to how they're marked on the template sheet.
5. Using the letters and flags as a guide, have them draw curves connecting the grid dots on at least one of the grids. The two "a" lines should be identical, as should the two "b" lines.
6. Have the students identify a motif in (one of) their shape(s). Then have them refine the shape and rough in interior details.
7. Have them further refine the shape and interior details to produce a prototile.
8. Have them cut out one curve of each type (one for each letter) and cut off the bulk of the sheet to create a template, as shown on the template sheet.
9. Have them use their templates to draw the outlines of the tiles on the Square Tessellation Grid sheet, as directed on the Template 8-2 sheet, continuing until the sheet is filled up.
10. Have them lightly sketch in key interior details for each tile.
11. Have the students use an ink pen to go over the tile outlines and interior details for the entire tessellation. After the ink is fully dry, unwanted pencil marks can be erased.
12. Have them color their tessellations. Before starting, you may wish to discuss coloring options.

Discussion Questions:
1. What motif did you use for your tile? Do you think it was effective? How would you change it if you could do it over again?
2. What step did you find the most challenging? Why?
3. Which tessellation with rotational symmetry do you like better, this one with tiles based on right triangles, or that used for Activity 7-2, with tiles based on squares? Why?

Activity 8-2. Creating a tessellation based on kite-shaped tiles

Materials: Copies of template sheet 8-4 on copier paper, Right Triangle and Kite Tile Grids sheet on card stock, Square Tessellation Grid sheet on a paper that can be drawn and colored on, scissors or craft knife, pencil, pen, eraser, crayons or colored pencils (or other means of coloring a tessellation).

Objective: Learn to create a tessellation by hand based on kite-shaped tiles.

Vocabulary: Kite-shaped tile.

Activity Sequence:
1. Write the vocabulary term on the board and discuss its meaning.
2. Pass out the copies and other materials.
3. On the bottom portion of the template sheet, have the students mark the lines of glide reflection symmetry, along with glide vectors that would cause the tessellation to perfectly overlie itself.
4. Have the students mark the letters and flags for each of the two kite tile grids in a similar fashion to how they're marked on the template sheet.
5. Using the letters and flags as a guide, have them draw curves connecting the grid dots on at least one of the grids. The two "a" lines should be mirror images of each other, as should the two "b" lines.
6. Have the students identify a motif in (one of) their shape(s). Then have them refine the shape and rough in interior details.
7. Have them further refine the shape and interior details to produce a prototile.
8. Have them cut out one curve of each type (one for each letter) and cut off the bulk of the sheet to create a template, as shown on the template sheet.
9. Have them use their templates to draw the outlines of the tiles on the Square Tessellation Grid sheet, as directed on the Template 8-4 sheet, continuing until the sheet is filled up.
10. Have them lightly sketch in key interior details for each tile.
11. Have the students use an ink pen to go over the tile outlines and interior details for the entire tessellation. After the ink is fully dry, unwanted pencil marks can be erased.
12. Have them color their tessellations. Before starting, you may wish to discuss coloring options.

Discussion Questions:
1. What motif did you use for your tile? Do you think it was effective? How would you change it if you could do it over again?
2. What step did you find the most challenging? Why?
3. Which tessellation with glide reflection symmetry do you like better, this one with tiles based on kites, or that used for Activity 7-3, with tiles based on squares? Why?

Tessellations Based on Equilateral Triangle Tiles

Tessellations based on equilateral triangle tiles are explored in this chapter. Unlike a regular tessellation of squares, a regular tessellation of equilateral triangles contains two different orientations of triangles, as shown below, related by a 180° rotation. For this reason, there is no single-prototile template that tessellates strictly by translational symmetry.

The fact that equilateral triangles appear in two orientations makes the grid a little more complicated than a square grid. However, tessellations based on equilateral triangles tend to be less static and more interesting than tessellations based on squares. Tiles based on equilateral triangles are particularly well-suited for tessellations with rotational symmetry, and the first template in this chapter has points of 2-, 3-, and 6-fold rotational symmetry.

M.C. Escher used tiles based on equilateral triangles in a number of his tessellations. Most of them haves birds and/or fish as the motifs. My personal experience is that distorting equilateral triangle tiles frequently creates tiles that suggest these creatures.

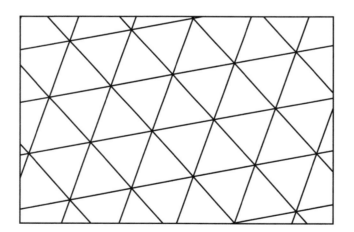

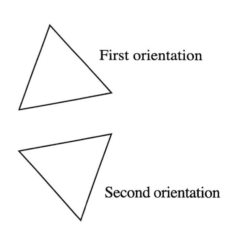

First orientation

Second orientation

Use these grids to design tiles using the templates found in Chapter 9. First choose a template, then copy the letters and flags for each line segment on a grid. Next, draw curves connecting the dots in a manner that follows the rules described by the letters and flags. Then cut out your tile as directed on the chosen template page, and follow the directions there to form a tessellation.

Tessellation with 6-fold rotational symmetry

This tessellation possesses points of 2-, 3-, and 6-fold rotational symmetry. The tile appears in six different orientations in the tessellation.

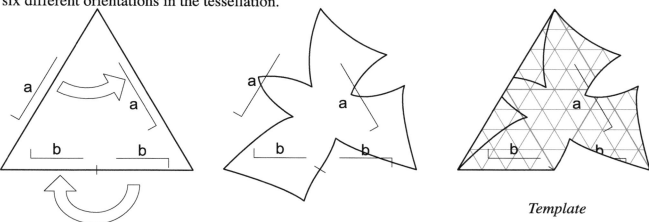

Template

To draw this tessellation using the grids:
To form your template, cut along the right edge and right half of the bottom edge of your tile, as shown. Form Line 1 by tracing along the cut edges. Then rotate your template 60° (1/6 of a full revolution) counter-clockwise and draw Line 2. Similarly draw Lines 3-6. To form a larger tessellation, repeat this group of six lines. The example below shows where to start your second group by drawing Line 7.

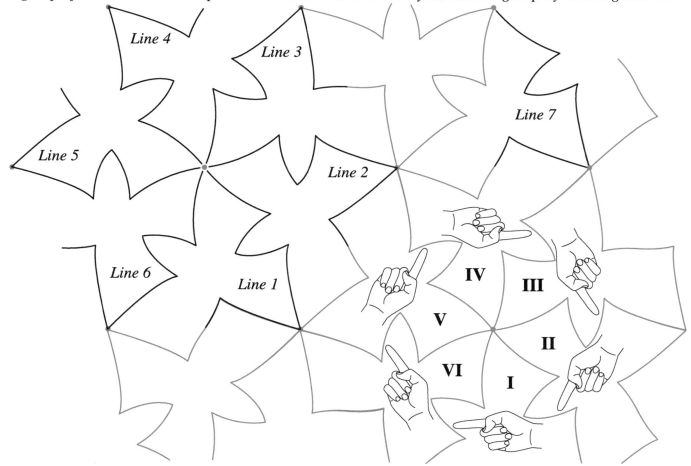

"Six-fold Seahorses"

This seahorse design is based on Template 9-1. Comparing this design to the 4-fold seahorse design on page 79 illustrates how the same motif can be distorted to change the symmetry of the tessellation. Try completing the seahorses in the top two rows of tiles.

Tessellation with rotational and glide reflection symmetry

This tessellations has both 2-fold rotational symmetry and glide reflection symmetry. The tile appears in four distinct orientations in the tessellations.

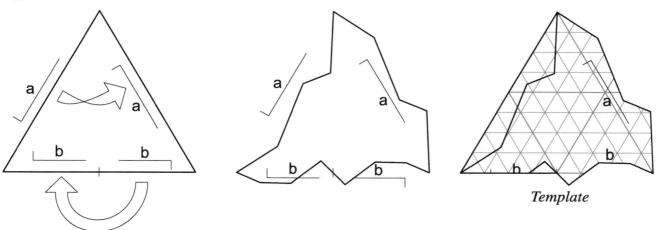

Template

To draw this tessellation using the grids:
To form your template, cut along the upper right curve a and the lower right curve b. Trace along these edges to draw Line 1 as shown below. Then rotate your template 180° (1/2 of a full revolution) and draw Line 2. Flip your template over left to right and draw Line 3. Then rotate 180° and draw Line 4. To form a larger tessellation, repeat this group of four lines as needed

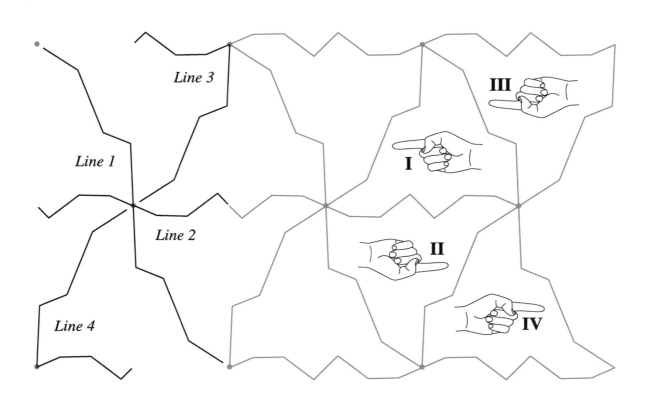

Tessellation with 2-fold rotational symmetry only

This tessellation has four distinct points of 2-fold rotational symmetry. The tile appears in two distinct orientations in the tessellation.

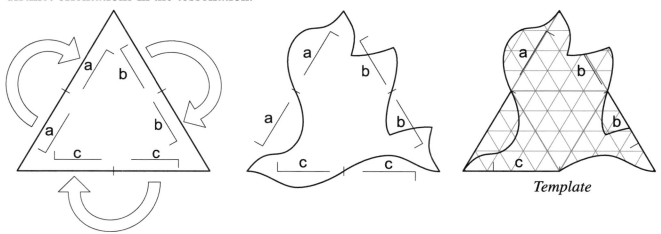

Template

To draw this tessellation using the grids:
To form your template, cut along three of the six curves making up your tile and cut the other three as straight lines, as shown above right. Form the first set of three lines by tracing the three curves with the template fixed in place. Then rotate the template 180° and form the second set of three lines, as shown below. Repeat this group of six lines to form a larger tessellation.

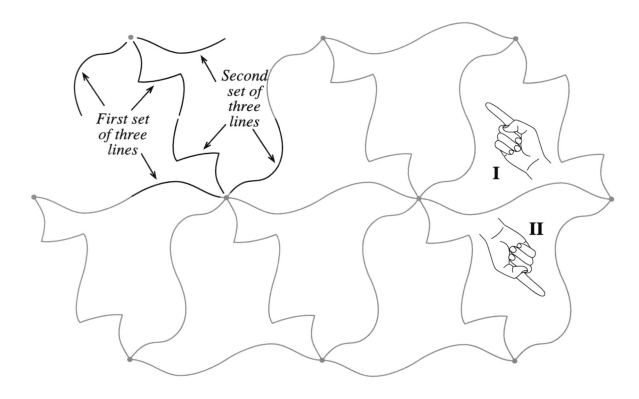

First set of three lines

Second set of three lines

I

II

Tessellation with translational symmetry only

This tessellation has two motifs, but only possesses translational symmetry.

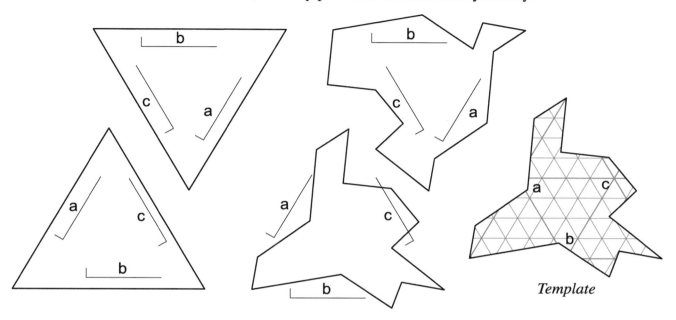

Template

To draw this tessellation using the grids:
To form your template, fully cut the lower of the two tiles. Trace around it to form a set of 3 lines. Reposition it as shown to form a second set of 3 lines. Repeat to form a larger tessellation.

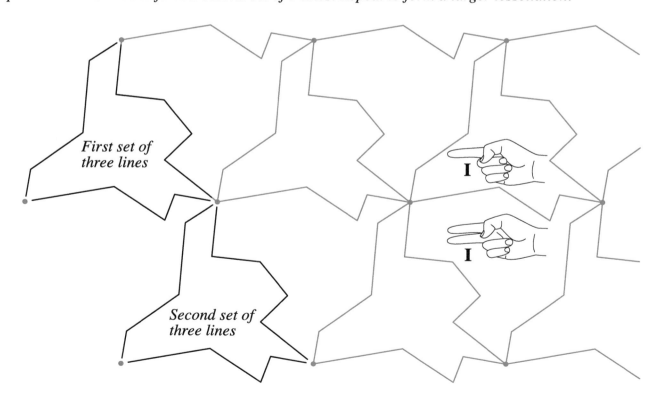

First set of three lines

Second set of three lines

Activity 9-1. Creating an equilateral-triangle-based tessellation with rotational symmetry

Materials: Copies of template sheet 9-1 on copier paper, copies of the Equilateral Triangle Tile Grids sheet on card stock, copies of the Equilateral Triangle Tessellation Grid sheet on a paper that can be drawn and colored on, scissors or craft knife, pencil, pen, eraser, crayons or colored pencils (or other means of coloring a tessellation).

Objective: Learn to create a tessellation by hand, based on an equilateral triangle tile, that possesses rotational symmetry.

Vocabulary: Equilateral triangle, n-fold rotational symmetry.

Activity Sequence:
1. Write the vocabulary terms on the board and discuss their meanings.
2. Pass out the copies and other materials.
3. On the bottom portion of the template sheet, have the students mark each distinct point of rotational symmetry, using a polygon to indicate the amount of rotation. For 2-fold rotation, use a rectangle. For 3-fold rotation, use a triangle. For 6-fold rotation, use a hexagon.
4. Have the students mark the letters and flags for each of the four Triangle Tile Grids in a similar fashion to how they're marked on the template sheet.
5. Using the letters and flags as a guide, have them draw curves connecting the grid dots on at least one of the grids. The two "a" lines should be identical, as should the two "b" lines.
6. Have the students identify a motif in (one of) their shape(s). Then have them refine the shape and rough in interior details.
7. Have them further refine the shape and interior details to produce a prototile.
8. Have them cut out one curve of each type (one for each letter) and cut off the bulk of the sheet to create a template, as shown on the template sheet.
9. Have them use their templates to draw the outlines of the tiles on the Equilateral Triangle Tessellation Grid sheet, as directed on the Template 9-1 sheet, continuing until the sheet is filled up.
10. Have them lightly sketch in key interior details for each tile.
11. Have the students use an ink pen to go over the tile outlines and interior details for the entire tessellation. After the ink is fully dry, unwanted pencil marks can be erased.
12. Have them color their tessellations. Before starting, you may wish to discuss coloring options.

Discussion Questions:
1. What motif did you use for your tile? Do you think it was effective? How would you change it if you could do it over again?
2. What step did you find the most challenging? Why?
3. Did you find designing this tessellation to be more or less difficult than designing a square tessellation with rotational symmetry (Activity 7-2)? Why?
4. Which of the two templates for tessellations possessing rotational symmetry, 7-2 or 9-1, do you like better? Why?

Activity 9-2. Creating an equilateral-triangle-based tessellation with glide reflection symmetry

Materials: Copies of template sheet 9-2 on copier paper, copies of the Equilateral Triangle Tile Grids sheet on card stock, copies of the Equilateral Triangle Tessellation Grid sheet on a paper that can be drawn and colored on, scissors or craft knife, pencil, pen, eraser, crayons or colored pencils (or other means of coloring a tessellation).

Objective: Learn to create a tessellation by hand, based on an equilateral triangle tile, that possesses glide reflection symmetry.

Vocabulary: Glide reflection symmetry.

Activity Sequence:
1. Write the vocabulary term on the board and discuss its meaning.
2. Pass out the copies and other materials.
3. On the bottom portion of the template sheet, have the students mark the lines of glide reflection symmetry, along with glide vectors that would cause the tessellation to perfectly overlie itself.
4. Have the students mark the letters and flags for each of the four Triangle Tile Grids in a similar fashion to how they're marked on the template sheet.
5. Using the letters and flags as a guide, have them draw curves connecting the grid dots on at least one of the grids. The two "b" lines should be identical, while the two "a" lines should be mirror images of each other.
6. Have the students identify a motif in (one of) their shape(s). Then have them refine the shape and rough in interior details.
7. Have them further refine the shape and interior details to produce a prototile.
8. Have them cut out one curve of each type (one for each letter) and cut off the bulk of the sheet to create a template, as shown on the template sheet.
9. Have them use their templates to draw the outlines of the tiles on the Equilateral Triangle Tessellation Grid sheet, as directed on the Template 9-2 sheet, continuing until the sheet is filled up.
10. Have them lightly sketch in key interior details for each tile.
11. Have the students use an ink pen to go over the tile outlines and interior details for the entire tessellation. After the ink is fully dry, unwanted pencil marks can be erased.
12. Have them color their tessellations. Before starting, you may wish to discuss coloring options.

Discussion Questions:
1. What motif did you use for your tile? Do you think it was effective? How would you change it if you could do it over again?
2. What step did you find the most challenging? Why?
3. Did you find designing this tessellation to be more or less difficult than designing the tessellation in Activities 9-1? Why?
4. Which of the two templates for tessellations possessing glide reflection symmetry, 7-3 or 9-2, do you like better? Why?

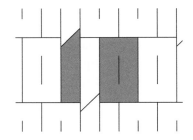

Tessellations Based on 60°-120° Rhombus Tiles

In this chapter some tessellations based on 60° - 120° rhombus tiles are described. These rhombi are made up of two equilateral triangles, as shown below left, and can be drawn on the Equilateral Triangle Tessellation Grid in Chapter 9. All of the rhombi are oriented the same, so tessellations possessing only translational symmetry are allowed. There are other ways of arranging the same rhombi. One possibility, which is used for Template 10-4, is shown below center. A third possibility, which is used for Templates 10-3 and 10-6, is shown below right.

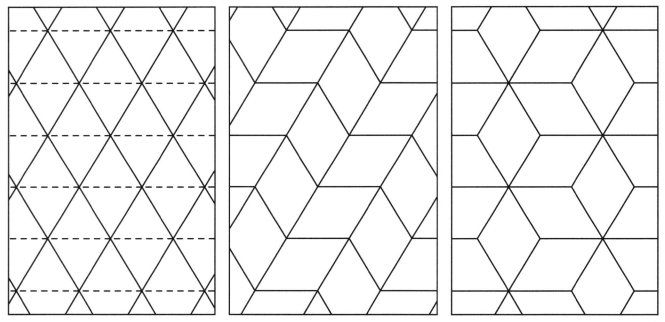

A rhombus has four sides of equal length, and two different interior angles. A square can be considered a special case of a rhombus in which all four interior angles are equal. Because they are closely related, some of the same Heesch types can be used as in Chapter 7. I.e., tessellations can be formed with the same symmetries. For example, Template 10-1 is the same Heesch type as Template 7-1, and can be considered a skewed version of Template 7-1.

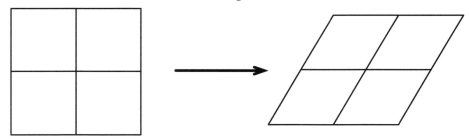

Use these grids to design tiles using the templates found in Chapter 10. First choose a template, then copy the letters and flags for each line segment on a grid. Next, draw curves connecting the dots in a manner that follows the rules described by the letters and flags. Then cut out your tile as directed on the chosen template page, and follow the directions there to form a tessellation.

Tessellation with translational symmetry only
Symmetry group p1, Heesch type TTTT

This is the simplest way to form a tessellation using an equilateral triangle grid. There are two independent line segments, each of which simply translates from one side of the rhombus to the other.

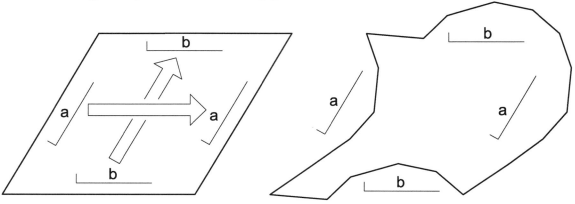

To draw this tessellation using the grids:
Cut along the top and right edges of your tile to form your template. Form Line 1 as indicated below by tracing the cut edges. Repeatedly form this same line in the same orientation to form a larger tessellation.

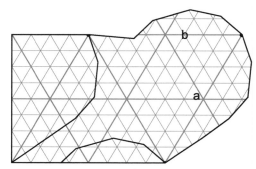

Template

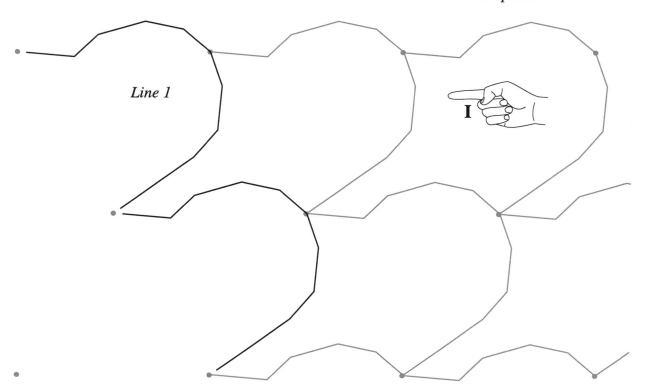

Line 1

I

"Manta Rays"

This design is based on Template 10-1. Try completing the rays at top.

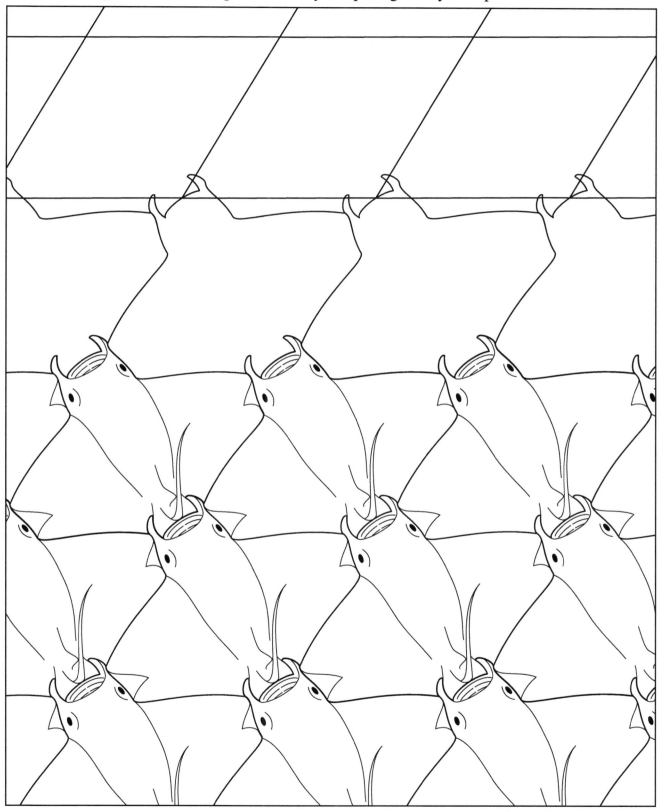

"Geese"

This geese design is also based on Template 10-1. Each rhombus is divided into two smaller tiles in this example, and the entire grid is rotated 30° clockwise, to make the geese level. Note that the two tiles have the same shape, but the interior details are different, so that all of the geese are right-side up, with half flying left to right, and half right to left. Try completing the geese at top.

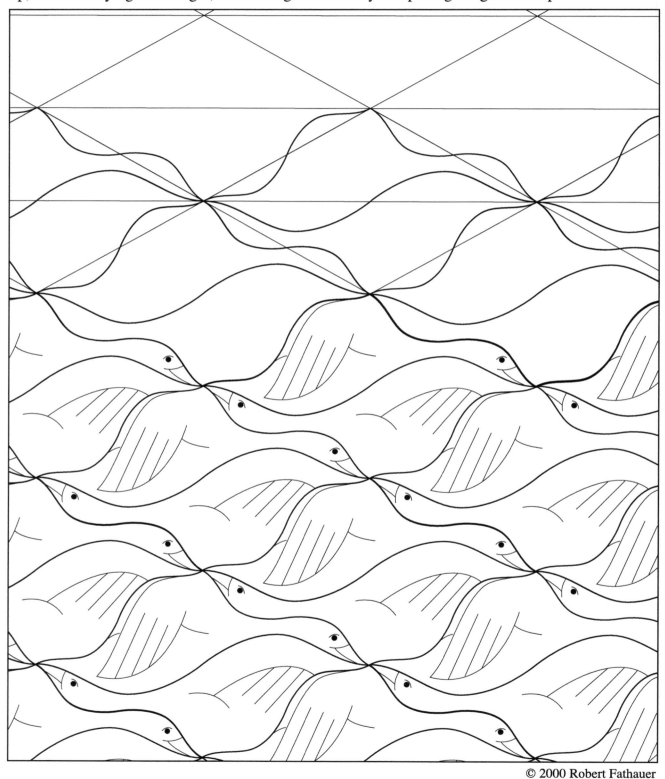

© 2000 Robert Fathauer

Tessellation with reflection symmetry
Symmetry group cm

This tessellation uses a single line segment four times to create a tile and a tessellation with reflection symmetry.

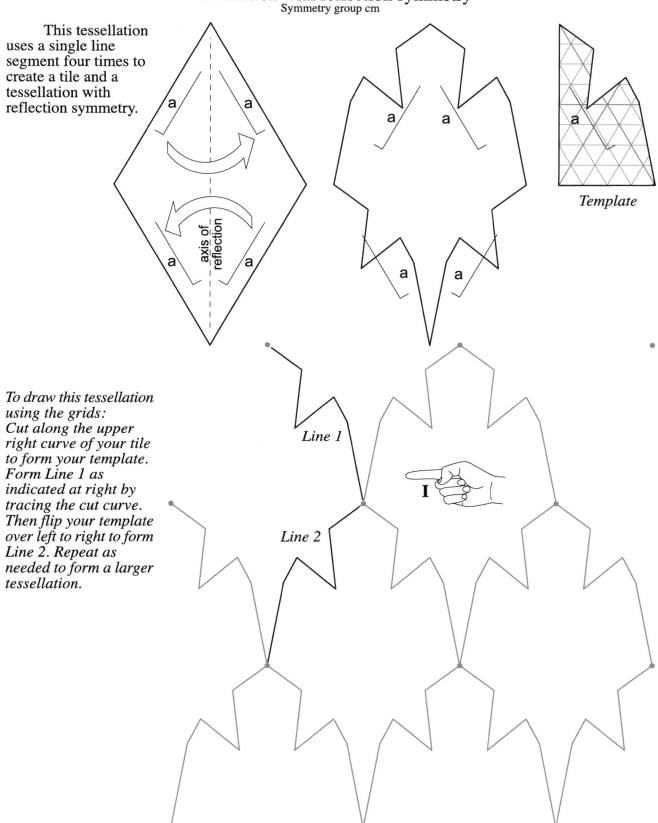

Template

To draw this tessellation using the grids: Cut along the upper right curve of your tile to form your template. Form Line 1 as indicated at right by tracing the cut curve. Then flip your template over left to right to form Line 2. Repeat as needed to form a larger tessellation.

axis of reflection

a a

a a

a a

a a

Line 1

Line 2

I

"Men in Coats"

This design is based on Template 10-2. Note that the interior details break the strict reflection symmetry. Try drawing in the interior details in the top tiles.

© 1990/2004 Robert Fathauer

Tessellation with 3-fold rotational symmetry

This template forms a tessellation with three distinct points of 3-fold rotational symmetry.

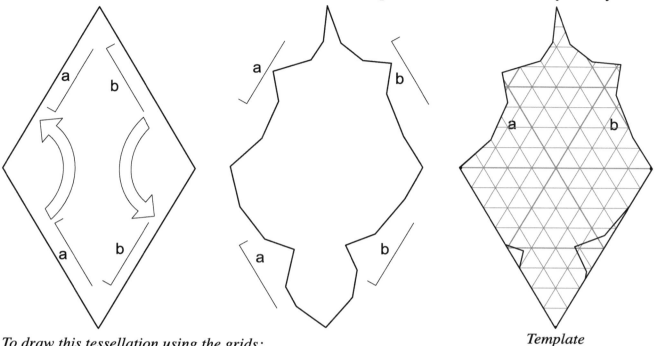

Template

To draw this tessellation using the grids:

Cut along the upper left and upper right edges of your tile to form your template. Form Line 1 as indicated below by tracing the cut edges. Rotate your template 120° counter-clockwise to draw Line 2. Rotate again to form Line 3. Repeatedly form this same group of three lines to form a larger tessellation.

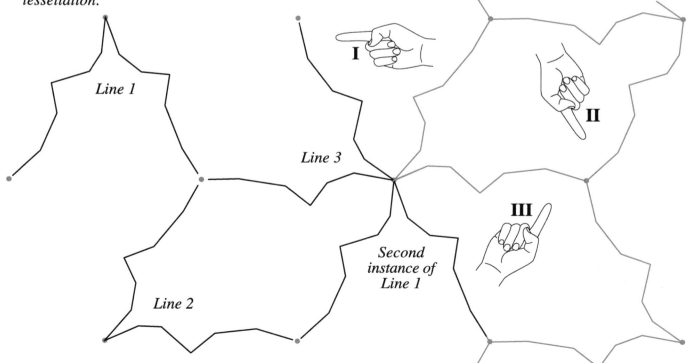

"Largemouth Bass"

This tessellation is based on Template 10-3. The triangular grid used here is smaller than the grid provided in Chapter 9. Notice how a line is used to move a portion of each tile away from a vertex. Try completing the drawing.

Template 10-4

Tessellation with glide reflection symmetry
Symmetry Group pg, Heesch type TGTG

This tessellation has two distinct lines of glide reflection symmetry. The tile appears in two distinct orientations.

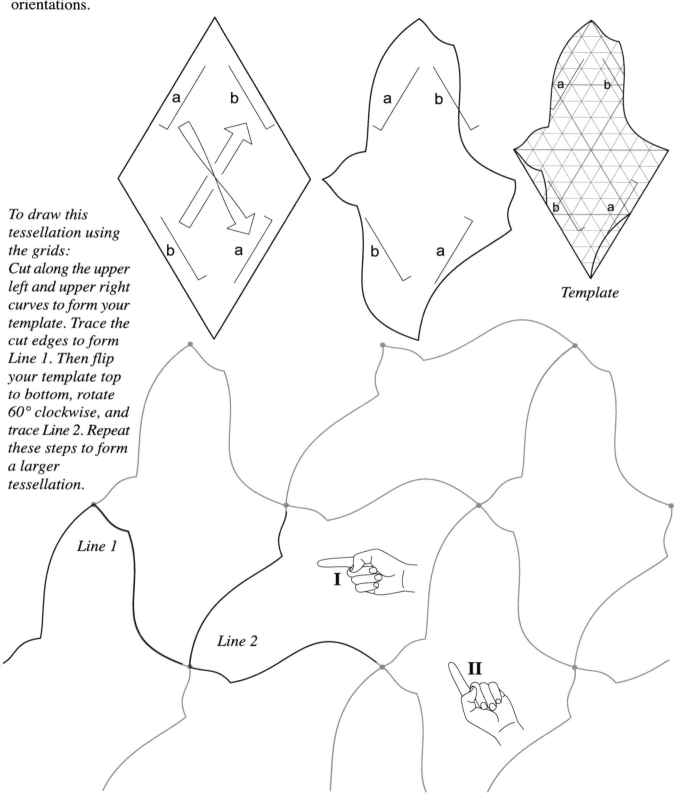

To draw this tessellation using the grids:
Cut along the upper left and upper right curves to form your template. Trace the cut edges to form Line 1. Then flip your template top to bottom, rotate 60° clockwise, and trace Line 2. Repeat these steps to form a larger tessellation.

Template

Line 1

Line 2

Tessellation with rotational and glide reflection symmetry

This tessellation uses a single line segment eight times to create two different tiles and a tessellation with reflection symmetry. The tiles in the top figure are shown smaller than the grid size due to space constraints.

To draw this tessellation using the grids:
Fully cut the lower of your two tiles. Trace around it to form a set of four lines. Flip your tile over top to bottom and trace around it to form a second set of four lines Repeat as needed to form a larger tessellation.

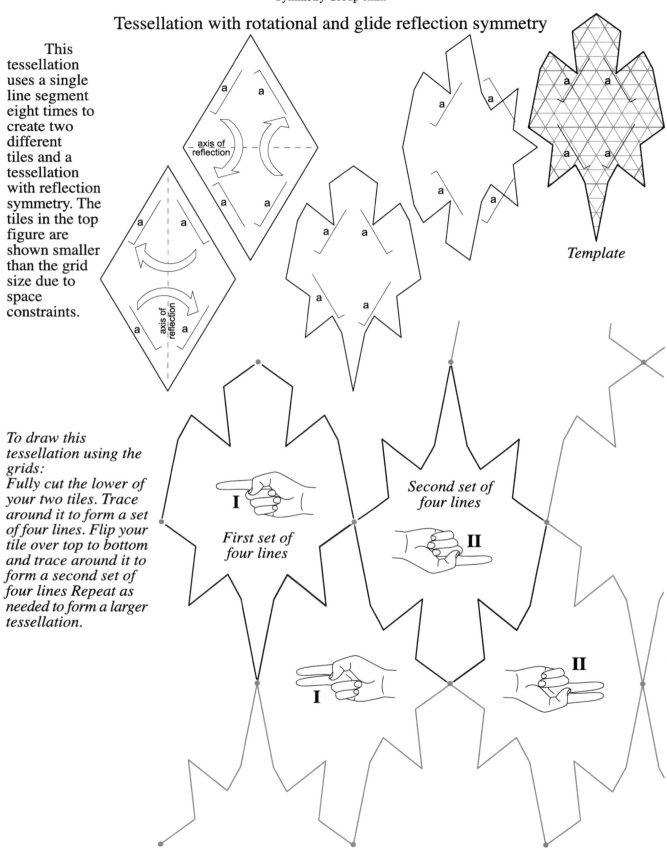

axis of reflection

axis of reflection

Template

First set of four lines

I

Second set of four lines

II

I

II

Tessellation with kaleidoscope symmetry

This template creates a tessellation with three different motifs and multiple lines of reflection symmetry. This sort of tessellation could be produced by a kaleidoscope with three mirrors arranged in an equilateral triangle, which is the most common type of kaleidoscope.

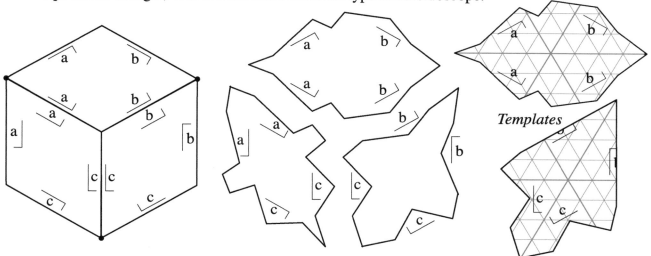

Templates

To draw a tessellation using the grids (Note – the Equilateral Triangle Tile Grids in Chapter 9 work better for this tessellation than the tile grids in this chapter):
Make two templates as shown. Trace completely around the top template to form Line 1. Rotate your template 120° clockwise to form Line 2, and again to form Line 3. Using the lower template, trace around the two cut "c" edges to form Line 4. Rotate your template 120° clockwise to form Line 5, and again to form Line 6. Repeat as needed to form a larger tessellation.

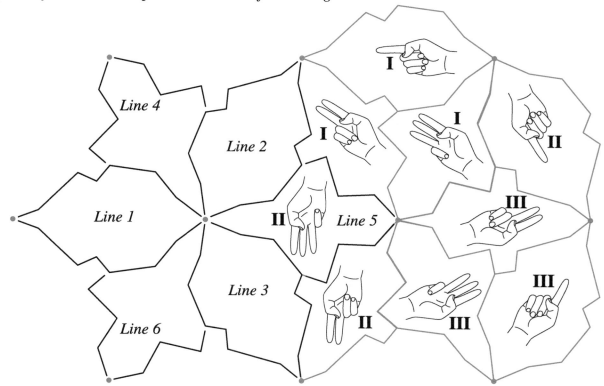

"Bug Reflections"

This design is based on Template 10-6. Try to complete the drawing at the top of the page.

Activity 10-1. Creating a tessellation with bilaterally-symmetric tiles

Materials: Copies of template sheet 10-2 on copier paper, copies of 60° - 120° Rhombus Tile Grids sheet on card stock, copies of Equilateral Triangle Tessellation Grid sheet on a paper that can be drawn and colored on, scissors or craft knife, pencil, pen, eraser, crayons or colored pencils (or other means of coloring a tessellation).

Objective: Learn to create a tessellation by hand, based on a 60° - 120° rhombus, that has bilaterally-symmetric tiles.

Vocabulary: Rhombus, bilateral symmetry.

Activity Sequence:
1. Write the vocabulary terms on the board and discuss their meanings.
2. Pass out the copies and other materials.
3. On the bottom portion of the template sheet, have the students mark the lines of reflection symmetry and lines of glide reflection symmetry, along with glide vectors that would cause the tessellation to perfectly overlie itself.
4. Have the students mark the letters and flags for each of the three Rhombus Tile Grids in a similar fashion to how they're marked on the template sheet.
5. Using the letters and flags as a guide, have them draw curves connecting the grid dots on at least one of the grids. Two of the four lines should be identical, and two should be mirror images of the other lines.
6. Have the students identify a motif in (one of) their shape(s). Then have them refine the shape and rough in interior details.
7. Have them further refine the shape and interior details to produce a prototile.
8. Have them cut out one curve and cut off the bulk of the sheet to create a template, as shown on the template sheet.
9. Have them use their templates to draw the outlines of the tiles on the Equilateral Triangle Tessellation Grid sheet, as directed on the Template 10-2 sheet, continuing until the sheet is filled up.
10. Have them lightly sketch in key interior details for each tile.
11. Have the students use an ink pen to go over the tile outlines and interior details for the entire tessellation. After the ink is fully dry, unwanted pencil marks can be erased.
12. Have them color their tessellations. Before starting, you may wish to discuss coloring options.

Discussion Questions:
1. What motif did you use for your tile? Do you think it was effective? How would you change it if you could do it over again?
2. Did you find designing this tessellation to be more or less difficult than designing the tessellations in earlier activities in which the tiles did not possess bilateral symmetry? Why?

Activity 10-2. Creating a tessellation with kaleidoscope symmetry

Materials: Template sheet 10-6 on copier paper, Equilateral Triangle Tile Grids sheet (Chapter 9) on card stock, Equilateral Triangle Tessellation Grid sheet on a paper that can be drawn and colored on, scissors or craft knife, pencil, pen, eraser, crayons or colored pencils (or other means of coloring a tessellation).

Objective: Learn to create a tessellation by hand, based on a 60° - 120° rhombus, that has three different tiles and kaleidoscope symmetry.

Vocabulary: kaleidoscope symmetry.

Activity Sequence:
1. Write the vocabulary term on the board and discuss its meaning. If possible, have the students look through a kaleidoscope to better understand the symmetry of this tessellation.
2. Pass out the copies and other materials.
3. On the bottom portion of the template sheet, have the students mark the lines of reflection symmetry, and points of rotational symmetry with equilateral triangles.
4. Have the students mark the letters and flags for each of the four Equilateral Triangle Tile Grids in a similar fashion to how they're marked on the template sheet. Turning the sheet upside down will orient the tile grids the same as the tiles on the Template sheet. Each tile grid will contain the set of three different prototiles that appear in the tessellation.
5. Using the letters and flags as a guide, have them draw curves to create a set of three tiles on at least one of the grids. Note that there are three distinct lines, each of which appears both in reflected and unreflected orientations.
6. Have the students identify motifs in one set of three shapes. Then have them refine the shapes and rough in interior details.
7. Have them further refine the shapes and interior details to produce a set of three prototiles.
8. Have them cut out one templates as directed on the template sheet.
9. Have them use their templates to draw the outlines of the tiles on the Equilateral Triangle Tessellation Grid sheet, as directed on the Template 10-6 sheet, continuing until the sheet is filled up.
10. Have them lightly sketch in key interior details for each tile.
11. Have the students use an ink pen to go over the tile outlines and interior details for the entire tessellation. After the ink is fully dry, unwanted pencil marks can be erased.
12. Have them color their tessellations. Before starting, you may wish to discuss coloring options.

Discussion Questions:
1. What motifs did you use for your tiles? Do the three motifs go together somehow? How would you change it if you could do it over again?
2. What sort of motifs do you think work well for a tessellation with kaleidoscope symmetry? Why?

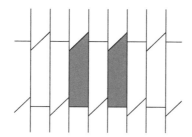

Tessellations Based on Hexagonal Tiles

In this chapter some tessellations based on hexagon and hexagram (a 6-pointed star polygon) tiles are described. These tessellations can be drawn on the Equilateral Triangle Tessellation Grid in Chapter 9. As described in Chapter 3, hexagons form the third regular tessellation. The other two, equilateral triangles and squares, were dealt with in Chapters 9 and 7, respectively.

A wide variety of tessellations may be formed using regular hexagons and hexagrams along with equilateral triangles. Some examples of tessellations incorporating regular hexagons and hexagrams are shown in Chapter 1 (Islamic art tessellations) and Chapter 3 (semi-regular and star-polygon tessellations), and additional examples are shown below.

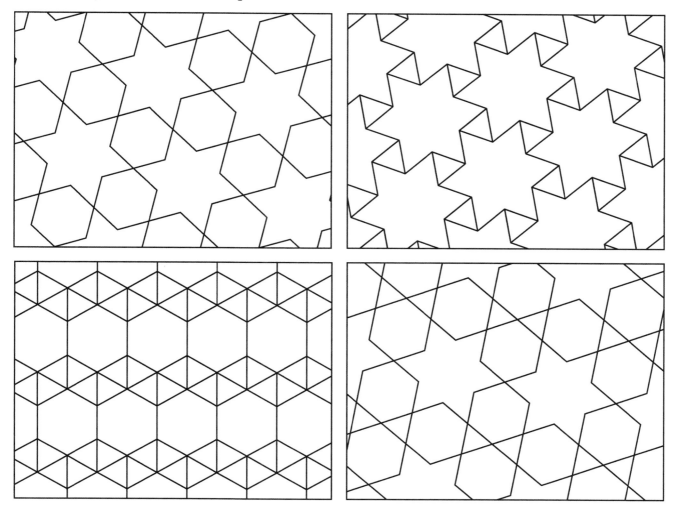

Use these grids to design tiles using the templates found in Chapter 11. First choose a template, then copy the letters and flags for each line segment on a grid. The short black lines show how the corners of hexagons and hexagrams fit on the grid. Draw curves connecting the corners of the tiles in a manner that follows the rules described by the letters and flags. Then cut out your tile as directed on the chosen template page, and follow the directions there to form a tessellation.

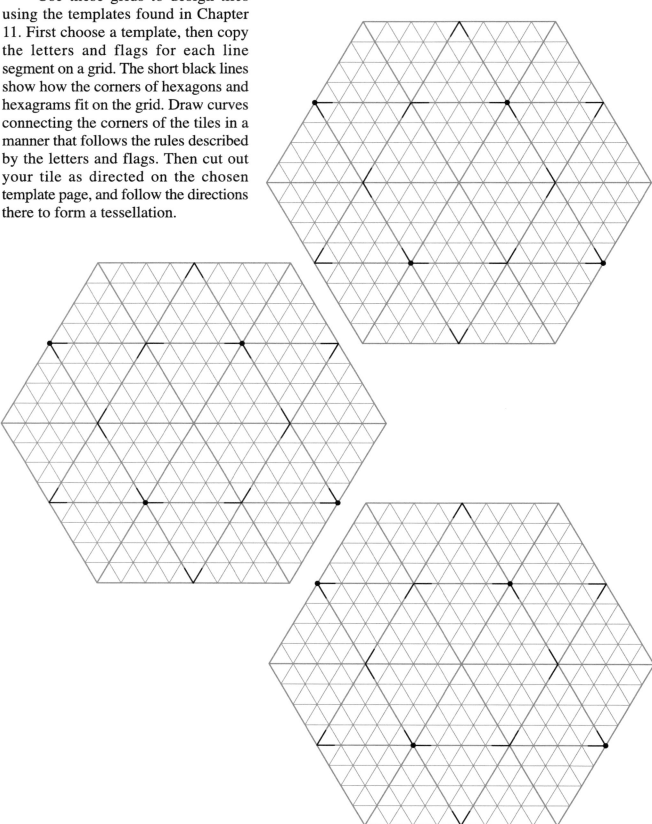

Tessellation with three-fold rotational symmetry

This tessellation has three distinct points of three-fold rotational symmetry, and the tile appears in three different orientations. This template can be used to create the tile that Escher used for his lizards that appear in the print *Reptiles*, which is similar to the example shown here.

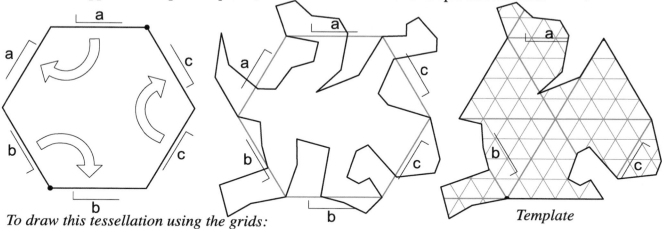

Template

To draw this tessellation using the grids:
Cut along three of the six curves making up your tile and cut the other three as straight lines, as shown above right. Form the first set of three lines by tracing the three curves with your template fixed in place. Then rotate the template 120° counter-clockwise and form the second set of three lines, as shown below, and another 120° to form the third set. Repeat this group of nine lines to form a larger tessellation.

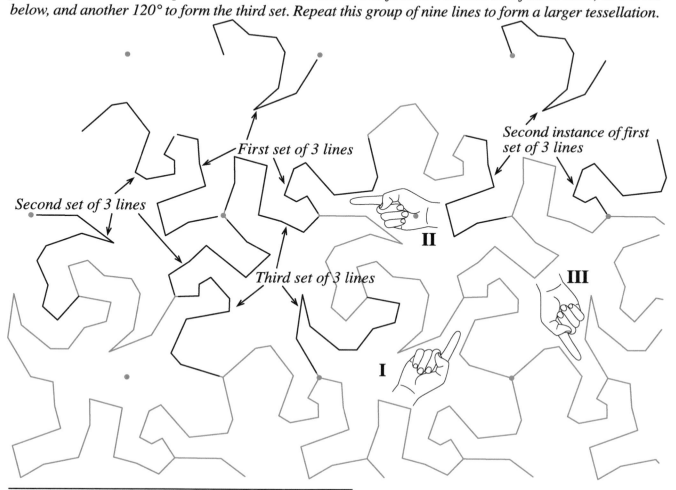

Tessellation with six-fold symmetric tiles

The tiles in this tessellation have 6-fold rotational symmetry. This sort of symmetry works well for snowflakes, starfish, flowers, and some other plants. A regular hexagon can be thought of as a group of six equilateral triangles. Using the triangles in the Equilateral Triangle Tessellation Grid would result in hexagons that are too big for tessellating on a single sheet of paper, so the hexagon here is half scale. For this reason, only two of the six corners will lie on black dots on the grid. This tessellation, with a prototile in which the same line segment appears 12 times, has points of 2-, 3-, and 6-fold rotational symmetry.

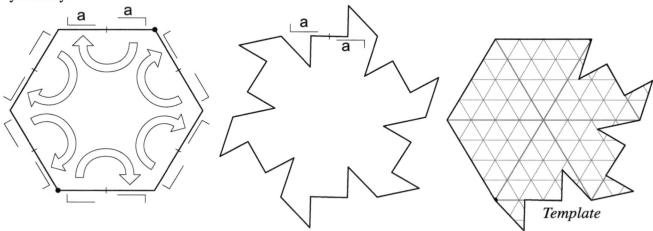

To draw a tessellation using the grids:
Make a template by cutting out half of a full tile, as shown. Draw Line 1 on the grid by tracing along the cut edges of your template. Translate your template to draw Lines 2-4. Note that each of the four lines match up to the dots on the grid differently. Repeat this group of four lines as needed to form a larger tessellation.

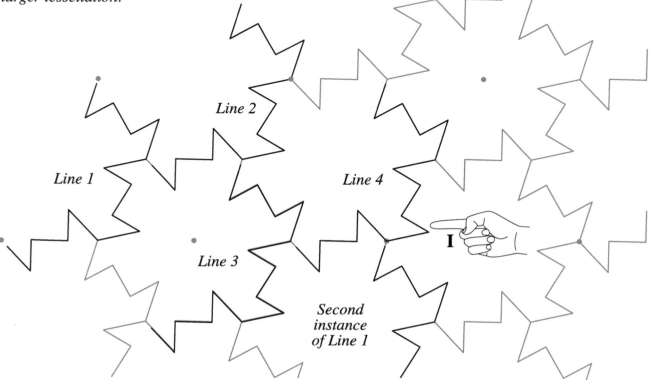

"Flowers II"

This design is based on Template 11-2. Can you identify the distinct points of 2-, 3-, and 6-fold rotational symmetry? Try completing the flowers at the top of the drawing.

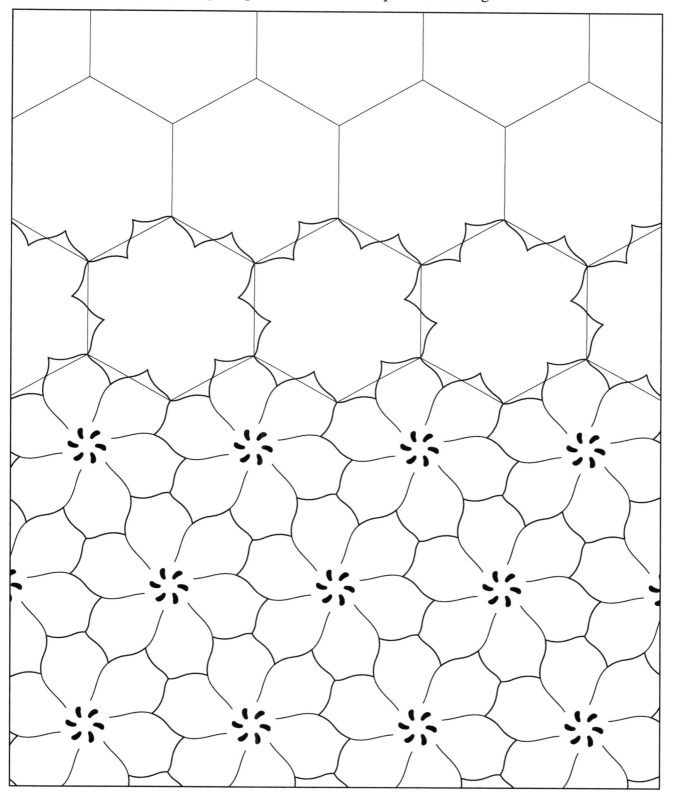

© 2006 Robert Fathauer

Tessellation based on hexagons and hexagrams

This template also works well for objects with 6-fold symmetry, but it has two prototiles, compared to the single prototile of Template 11-2. One is a regular hexagon, and the other is a hexagram. The left and middle figures below are reduced in size to fit better on the page, but the template is full size.

Template

To draw a tessellation using the grids:
Completely cut out the smaller tile to form your template, as shown. Trace all the way around your template to form Line 1. Translate your template to draw Line 2. Repeat this group of two lines as needed to form a larger tessellation.

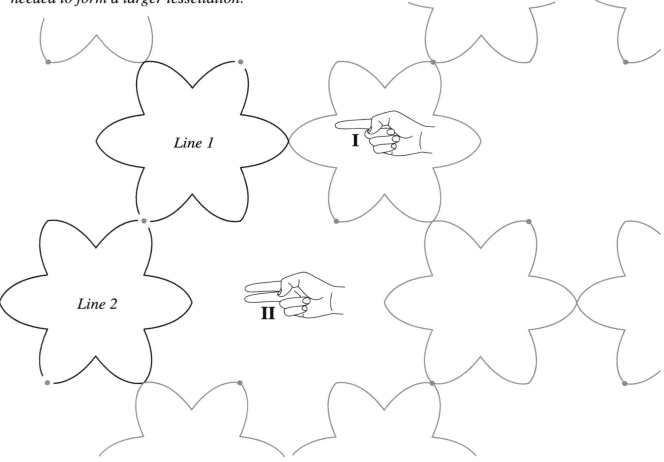

"Snowflakes"

This design is based on Template 11-3. Try drawing your own interior details in the top tiles.

Activities

Activity 11-1. Creating a tessellation based on hexagonal tiles

Materials: Template sheet 11-1 on copier paper, Hexagon Tile Grids sheet on card stock, Equilateral Triangle Tessellation Grid sheet on a paper that can be drawn and colored on, scissors or craft knife, pencil, pen, eraser, crayons or colored pencils (or other means of coloring a tessellation).

Objective: Learn to create a tessellation by hand, based on a hexagonal tile, that has 3-fold rotational symmetry.

Vocabulary: hexagonal tile, corners of a tile.

Activity Sequence:
1. Write the vocabulary terms on the board and discuss their meanings.
2. Pass out the copies and other materials.
3. On the bottom portion of the template sheet, have the students mark each distinct point of three-fold rotational symmetry with a triangle.
4. Have the students mark the letters and flags for each of the three Hexagon Tile Grids in a similar fashion to how they're marked on the template sheet.
5. Using the letters and flags as a guide, have them draw curves connecting the corners of the tiles on at least one of the grids. The two "a" lines should be identical, as should the two "b" lines and "c" lines.
6. Have the students identify a motif in (one of) their shape(s). Then have them refine the shape and rough in interior details.
7. Have them further refine the shape and interior details to produce a prototile.
8. Have them cut out one curve of each type (one for each letter) and cut off the bulk of the sheet to create a template, as shown on the template sheet.
9. Have them use their templates to draw the outlines of the tiles on the Equilateral Triangle Tessellation Grid sheet, as directed on the Template 11-1 sheet, continuing until the sheet is filled up.
10. Have them lightly sketch in key interior details for each tile.
11. Have the students use an ink pen to go over the tile outlines and interior details for the entire tessellation. After the ink is fully dry, unwanted pencil marks can be erased.
12. Have them color their tessellations. Before starting, you may wish to discuss coloring options.

Discussion Questions:
1. What motif did you use for your tile? Do you think it was effective? How would you change it if you could do it over again?
2. What step did you find the most challenging? Why?
3. Which of the three templates for tessellations possessing rotational symmetry, 7-2, 9-1, or 11-1, do you like the best? Why?

Activity 11-2. Creating a hexagon-based tessellation with 2-, 3-, and 6-fold rotational symmetry

Materials: Template sheet 11-2 on copier paper, Hexagon Tile Grids sheet on card stock, Equilateral Triangle Tessellation Grid sheet on a paper that can be drawn and colored on, scissors or craft knife, pencil, pen, eraser, crayons or colored pencils (or other means of coloring a tessellation).

Objective: Learn to create a tessellation by hand, based on a hexagonal tile, that has 2-, 3-, and 6-fold rotational symmetry.

Vocabulary: hexagonal tile, n-fold rotational symmetry, corners of a tile.

Activity Sequence:
1. Write the vocabulary terms on the board and discuss their meanings.
2. Pass out the copies and other materials.
3. On the bottom portion of the template sheet, have the students mark each point of two-fold rotational symmetry with a rectangle, each point of three-fold rotational symmetry with a triangle, and each point of six-fold rotational symmetry with a hexagon.
4. Have the students mark the letters and flags for each of the three Hexagon Tile Grids in a similar fashion to how they're marked on the template sheet. Also have them make tick marks half-way along each edge of the hexagon.
5. Using the letters, flags, and tick marks as a guide, have them draw curves connecting the corners of the tiles on at least one of the grids. Each edge of the hexagon should have two short "a" lines that are related by a 180° rotation about a tick mark.
6. Have the students identify a motif in (one of) their shape(s). Then have them refine the shape and rough in interior details.
7. Have them further refine the shape and interior details to produce a prototile.
8. Have them cut out half of a full tile to create a template, as shown on the template sheet.
9. Have them use their templates to draw the outlines of the tiles on the Equilateral Triangle Tessellation Grid sheet, as directed on the Template 11-2 sheet, continuing until the sheet is filled up.
10. Have them lightly sketch in key interior details for each tile.
11. Have the students use an ink pen to go over the tile outlines and interior details for the entire tessellation. After the ink is fully dry, unwanted pencil marks can be erased.
12. Have them color their tessellations. Before starting, you may wish to discuss coloring options.

Discussion Questions:
1. What motif did you use for your tile? Do you think it was effective? How would you change it if you could do it over again?
2. What step did you find the most challenging? Why?
3. In Activity 9-1, a different tessellation with 2-, 3-, and 6-fold symmetry was created. Which of the two do you like better? Why?

Bibliography

Jill Britton, *Symmetry and Tessellations*, White Plains, New York, Dale Seymour Publications, 2000.

F.H. Bool, J.R. Kist, J.L. Locher, and F. Wierda, *M. C. Escher – His Life and Complete Graphic Work*, New York, Harry N. Abrams, 1982.

Issam El-Said and Ayse Parman, *Geometric Concepts in Islamic Art*, Palo Alto, Dale Seymour Publications, 1990.

Branko Grünbaum and G.C. Shephard, *Tilings and Patterns*, New York, W.H. Freeman and Company, 1987.

Koloman Moser, *Turn-of-the-century Viennese Patterns and Designs*, Mineola, New York, Dover Publications, 1998.

Doris Schattschneider, *Visions of Symmetry – Notebooks, Drawings, and Related Works of M. C. Escher*, New York, W.H. Freeman and Company, 2004.

Doris Schattschneider and Wallace Walker, *M. C. Escher Kaleidocycles*, Petaluma, California, Pomegranate Communications, 2003.

Dale Seymour and Jill Britton, *Introduction to Tessellations*, Palo Alto, California, Dale Seymour Publications, 1989.

Pam Stephens and Jim McNeill, *Tessellations – The History and Making of Symmetrical Designs*, Aspen, Colorado, Crystal Productions, 2001.

Websites Featuring Tessellation Art

(Artist, followed by url. This is a small sampling of artists and websites. Additional artists can be found on the websites of Andrew Crompton and Patrick Snels.)

David Bailey, http://www.tess-elation.co.uk/.

Andrew Crompton, http://www.cromp.com/tess/home.html.

Hop David, http://www.tabletoptelephone.com/~hopspage/HopsTiles.html.

Robert Fathauer, http://members.cox.net/fathauerart/index.html.

Ken Landry, http://www.landryart.com/.

Jim McNeill, http://www.jimmcneill.com/.

Makoto Nakamura, http://www.k4.dion.ne.jp/~mnaka/home.index.html.

John Osborn, http://www.ozbird.net/.

Peter Raedschelders, http://home.scarlet.be/~praedsch/.

Dominque Ribault, http://www.polytess.info/. (Note to teachers – this site contains nudes.)

Patrick Snels, http://tessellation.info/.

Glossary

Angle: a measure of the amount of turning necessary to bring a line or other object into coincidence with another.

Bilateral symmetry: a symmetry in which two halves of an object mirror each other about a center line.

Coloring (of a tessellation): how colors are assigned to the different tiles in a tessellation.

Corner (of a tile): a point where two edges of a tile meet.

Dart: a quadrilateral with two adjacent sides of one length and two other adjacent side of a second length, and one interior angle greater than 180°.

Dodecagon: a 12-sided polygon.

Edge (of a tile): a portion of the boundary of a tile, linking two corners of the tile.

Edge-to-edge (tessellation): one in which the corners of the tiles correspond to vertices of the tessellation.

Equilateral triangle: a triangle in which each side is of the same length and all three interior angles measure 60°.

Escheresque tile: a tile that resembles a real-world motif; in a general sense, the sort of tiles found in the tessellations for which M.C. Escher is famous.

Escheresque tessellation (or tiling): a tessellation in which the tiles are Escheresque, resembling real-world motifs.

Figure: the part of a scene or drawing that is in the foreground, usually representing a form or forms.

Geometric tessellation: a tessellation in which the individual tiles are geometric shapes as opposed to real-world motifs.

Glide reflection: a motion consisting of a translation and a reflection or mirroring.

Glide-reflection symmetry: the property of not changing under some combined translation and reflection.

Ground: the part of a scene or drawing that is in the background, usually space around and behind a form or forms.

Heesch type: a classification system for tiles that will tessellate, due to Heinrich Heesch.

Hexagon: a 6-sided polygon.

Hexagram: a 6-pointed star polygon with alternating interior angles of 60° and 240°.

Infinite: endless, extending indefinitely.

Interior details (of a tile): lines, dots, shading, etc of the interior of a tile, used to suggest a real-world motif.

Isosceles triangle: a triangle in which two of the sides are equal in length. An isosceles right triangle is an isosceles triangle containing a right angle; i.e., one with angles 90°, 45°, and 45°.

Kaleidoscope symmetry: the property of not changing under a set of reflections such as those observed in a kaleidoscope.

Kite: a quadrilateral with two adjacent sides of one length and two other adjacent sides of a second length, and all angles less than 180°.

Mathematical modeling: the use of mathematics to approximate and better understand the physical world.

Mathematical plane: a theoretical flat (2-dimensional) surface extending to infinity in all directions.

Mirror symmetry: the property of not changing under a reflection.

Motif: a theme or subject.

Natural tessellation: one found in nature. Natural tessellations are always approximate and finite in extent.

Non-periodic tessellation: one that doesn't repeat; i.e., one not possessing translational symmetry.

Octagon: an 8-sided polygon.

Orientation: the way in which an object is aligned with respect to it's surroundings.

Parallelogram: a quadrilateral in which both pairs of opposing sides are parallel. A rhombus is a special case of a parallelogram.

Pentagon: a 5-sided polygon.

Polygon: a closed plane figure made up of straight-line segments.

Polygonal tile: one in which the edges are all straight lines.

Polyomino: a shape made of squares connected in edge-to-edge fashion.

Prototile: a tile to which many or all other tiles in a tessellation are similar.

Quadrilateral: a four-sided polygon.

Realistic drawing: one in which objects are drawn to resemble real-world objects as nearly as possible.

Rectangle: a quadrilateral in which every angle is 90°. A square is a special case of a rectangle.

Reflection: a transformation in which each point is replaced by a point at the opposite position with respect to a line or plane, as if by a mirror.

Regular polygon: one in which each side is of the same length and each interior angle of the same measure.

Regular tessellation: an edge-to-edge tessellation for which each tile is the same type of regular polygon.

Rhombus: a quadrilateral in which every side is of the same length.

Right triangle: one that contains a 90° angle.

Rotation: a turning about a point (in two dimensions) or a line (in three dimensions).

Rotational symmetry: the property of not changing under some rotation, or turning.

Semi-regular tessellation: an edge-to-edge tessellation for which every tile is a regular polygon, there are at least two different regular polygons, and each vertex is of the same type.

Skew: to distort an object such that all points on one axis remain fixed, and other points are shifted parallel to that axis by a distance proportional to their perpendicular distance from the axis. Another word for skew is shear.

Source material: items, such as photographs and illustrations, used as reference material to assist in the creation of a drawing, etc.

Star polygon: one in which the interior angles alternate between being greater than 180° and less than <180°.

Stylized drawing: one in which objects are intentionally drawn in a manner or style that doesn't conform to the real world.

Symmetry: the property of not changing under some transformation.

Symmetry group: a classification of a two-dimensional pattern based on the symmetries in the pattern.

Tessellation: a collection of shapes (tiles) that fit together without gaps or overlaps to cover the mathematical plane.

Tessera: a small square or cube of stone or glass used for making mosaics.

Tile: a set in the plane whose boundary is a single simple closed curve; the building block of tessellations.

Tiling: a collection of shapes (tiles) that fit together without gaps or overlaps to cover the mathematical plane.

Transformation: the changing from one configuration into another.

Translation: a movement in some direction by some amount with rotating or reflecting.

Translational symmetry: the property of not changing under some movement that is free of rotation or reflection.

Trapezoid: a quadrilateral in which one pair of opposing sides are parallel.

Utilitarian: of practical use.

Unit cell: the smallest group of tiles in a tessellation that may be repeatedly copied and used to generate the entire tessellation through translation only.

Vertex: a point at which three or more tiles meet.

Viewpoint: point of view; position from which something is looked at.

General Index

Index of Tessellation Motifs

(in original designs by the author)

Selected Tessellations Products

These products are produced by Tessellations, Robert Fathauer's company. More information on these products may be found at www.tessellations.com.

Tessellation Puzzles – Each puzzle contains foam tiles that can be assembled in many different ways, encouraging creativity, and exploration of symmetry and other math concepts.

In the Garden. Features 6 different things you might find in a garden.

In the Garden Too. Companion set to *In the Garden*, includes 6 additional things you might find in a garden.

Kites & Darts. Aperiodic tessellation set based on the Penrose tiles.

Out in Space. Includes the sun, planets, astronauts and the Space Shuttle, plus asteroids and glow-in-the-dark comets and stars. The tiles are based on regular polygons.

Squids & Rays. Features squids and rays based on rhombi.

Tessel-gons. Contains equilateral triangles, squares, regular hexagons, octagons, and dodecagons.

Tessel-gon Stars. Contains equilateral triangles, squares, and star polygons with three, four, six, eight, and twelve points.

Classroom Posters – 22" x 34" posters that include worksheets.

Regular Polygon Tessellations. Shows 18 tessellations of regular polygons, including the 3 regular and 8 semi-regular tessellations.

Symmetry in Tessellations. Shows 11 Escheresque tessellations and describe the different types of symmetry found in tessellations.

Tessellations in Our World. Shows 9 examples of tessellations in natural and manmade objects.

Activity Books – Each contains 30 different tessellations, with 5 activities for each tessellation.

Regular Polygon Tessellations. Features tessellations of regular polygons.

Lifelike Tessellations. Features Escheresque tessellations.